SONNY **ROLLINS**:
The Cutting Edge

Other titles in the **EastNote** series

Artie**Shaw**: Non-Stop Flight - John White
Jan**Garbarek:** Deep Song - Michael Tucker

forthcoming

Bill**Evans**: - Keith Shadwick
Oscar**Peterson:** Discography - Arnold van Kampen

Series Editor - Richard Palmer

SONNY**ROLLINS**:
The Cutting Edge

Richard Palmer

EastNote

This book is dedicated to Michael Tucker & John White

EastNote

HULL STUDIES IN JAZZ

The University of Hull Press
Cottingham Road
Hull
HU6 7RX

A CIP catalogue record for this book is available from the British Library.

Published 1998

Paperback ISBN 0 85958 667 7

Printed by LSL Press, Bedford, England

All photographs appear courtesy of Peter Symes

CONTENTS

Acknowledgements

The work of Sonny Rollins has inspired a good deal of excellent analysis and observation, and I owe a particular debt to the work of Gary Giddins, Ira Gitler, Joe Goldberg, Barry McRae and the late Martin Williams. I would also like to thank Raymond Horricks for the loan of some important material; Eddie Cook and *Jazz Journal International* for enabling me regularly to review Rollins records; Michael Shera for his encouragement and many telling insights; Peter Symes for his photographs and Ken Rattenbury for his transactions; and, as always, my wife Annie, not least for her loving forbearance during the manuscript's composition.

Above all, however, I want to express my gratitude to Michael Tucker and John White – for their stimulating ideas and discussion, their generous loan of recordings and written material, and their invaluable editorial suggestions. It is a privilege to dedicate a book to two such friends; needless to say, its surviving shortcomings are no fault of theirs.

Preface

The titans of the tenor saxophone have nearly all been taken from us. Lester Young died in 1959; John Coltrane in 1967; Coleman Hawkins the year after that and Ben Webster in 1973; and Stan Getz in 1991. Only one indisputably great jazz tenorist remains: Theodore Walter 'Sonny' Rollins.

Throughout his career he has been committed to the fundamental truths of jazz, especially swing. At the same time he has managed to be consistently experimental and forward-looking; his changes of direction have been as momentous as well-publicised, and his recorded *oeuvre* includes well over a dozen albums essential to any serious collection. He was the first – and the best – of those who sought to marry the rhythmic and harmonic innovations of Charlie Parker to the values embodied by Hawkins and Young, and he also developed Parker's revolutionary intimations to the full, particularly in matters of structure and shape.

Yet Rollins is an enigmatic figure whose six-decade career is difficult to evaluate. As a quick glance at the Bibliography will indicate, he has been much discussed; yet although those appraisals are invariably admiring, there is no obvious consensus about his work – about precisely why he is a great jazzman, what are his best records, what have been his most successful periods of activity, and so on. There is a particular divergence of opinion concerning the two-year 'sabbatical' that Rollins took between 1959 and 1961. Some think this complete break from gigs and recording revivified him, facilitating a change in direction as influential as personally triumphant; others find that subsequent work intermittently satisfying at best, evidence of a decline both in aesthetic quality and pioneering significance. And his 70s, 80s and 90s work, following another extended furlough in the late 60s, has provoked equally differing responses. Some consider his use of rock rhythms and fusion material a sad trivialization of his talent and the formidable achievements of his earlier years while many others have welcomed it as evidence of a new serenity and a now-consistent musical approach.

In addition, several highly experienced and knowledgeable *aficionados* argue that Rollins 'live' is a different animal from Rollins the studio artist, and that even his greatest records do not tell the full story. Given that this book is a critical and discographical account of Rollins's career rather than any kind of attempt at intimate biography, that is a major issue. I address it in full in Part Four; here I will merely telegraph two considerations, both large and both problematic. First, audiences are as various in a club or an auditorium as gathered round stereo equipment in a living room, and however eloquent may be the testaments of those who champion Rollins's 'live' superiority, one finally has only their word for it. Second, the entire jazz art dramatises a conflict between existentialism and durability – or to put it in more everyday terms, between 'live' spontaneity and organised preservation. While Rollins is a peculiarly charismatic protagonist in that drama, his career offers no decisive resolution of a debate that has raged ever since jazz's inception. The only certain thing is that when we're all dead and gone – writer, subject and readers – the records will be all that is left.

My detailed views on these and other matters will become clear as my account unfolds; for now I wish to make one more preliminary observation. After immersing myself in the many articles on Rollins and numerous interviews with him, my strongest impression is of a bewildering diffidence. Throughout his career he has been bothered by what critics and other musicians think about him – not 'upset' in the obvious sense, but invaded and disturbed by their appraisal. In addition, he has often felt pressured by other jazzmen's work, worrying about their achievements and choices of direction, as if they make him wonder if his own ways are right after all.

Why should this be "bewildering"? Should it not be argued instead that such humility, openness and desire to learn are wholly admirable? Well, yes; yet it strikes me that Rollins has often lacked his proper share of vanity and confidence in his gifts – a lack deeply at odds with the blistering panache of so much of his playing. To explore that paradox I turn in brief comparison to his virtual contemporary, Stan Getz.

Even before Donald L. Maggin's harrowing biography of Getz appeared in 1996[1], the tenorist was known to have been 'difficult'. Recent chapter and verse have been provided by film director Arthur Penn, with whom Getz worked on the soundtrack for *Mickey One* -

> He was burry as a cactus. Tough to handle, easily frustrated. When he would get in the groove he would be fabulous. When things did not go right he would be just mean.[2]

- and Creed Taylor, Getz's producer at Verve throughout the 1960s, whose words have an ominous economy: "Stan was always Stan."[3]

The point here is that there was always a striking disparity between the beauty of Getz's music and his usual behaviour as a human being. Maggin's work has dramatised that polarity in almost shocking detail; he has found a warm champion in the noted Getz scholar Ron Kirkpatrick, who argues that

> In presenting us with such a stark and harrowing picture of Getz's inability to cope with life at the personal level, usually resulting in his striking out at those nearest and dearest to him, Maggin offers us the opportunity to identify with a difficulty we all experience from time to time, and thus better our understanding. Unfortunately for Getz this problem assumed gigantic proportions, but then so did his genius.[4]

Essentially the same point is made, albeit in a different way, by Melvyn Bragg towards the end of his 1997 essay, "Must We Learn to Hate Norman Mailer?". He observes that "The list of flawed, damaged and nasty artists is very long," and concludes

> The work must stand aside from the life. It can be mixed up with it for the enjoyment of biography, but in the end it is something else. It belongs to a different category. The work is not the property of the life but finally a gift to our common imagination.[5]

All that is unquestionably true; furthermore, for all those of us who were never involved with or part of "the life", the work is far more important, which is one of several significant judgments implicit in D.H. Lawrence's maxim, "Never trust the artist. Trust the tale."[6] Yet in returning to and delivering the comparison originally outlined, it crosses my mind sometimes that it would make more sense if Rollins the man sounded like Getz the tenorist, and *vice versa*. To listen to the Getz of *Her* (on **Focus**) or *O Grande Amor* (on **Sweet Rain**) just after reading certain parts of Maggin's biography can be an unnerving, even surreal experience.[7] And if the Rollins-converse is not so extreme, it is hardly less startling at times. There is nothing "burry-cactus"-like about his tone, especially during the 1950s, nor (*pace* some commentators) is his music ever violent or angry; it does nevertheless have a masculine swagger and edge strongly reminiscent of Coleman Hawkins, and that is at odds with many aspects of his nature.

The contrast with Getz is instructive in less dramatic ways too. No matter what the prevailing fashion, Getz was always sure of what he wanted to do musically and had the firmest confidence in his own judgment. One of his last albums was called **Serenity**,[8] and whatever his private vicissitudes and "inability to cope with life at the personal level", the noun is an apposite summary of his artistic assurance throughout his career. Rollins is every bit Getz's equal as an improviser – some would say manifestly superior, if only because he was from the start ideologically committed to improvisation-as-experiment in a way that never quite characterised Getz. But that healthy inquisitiveness has more than once declined into mere restlessness, leading to a lack of clarity about what he really wanted to do musically.

It would of course be idiotic to suggest that either Getz or Rollins was a 'better player' than the other; the only sensible thing to say is that we are fortunate to have had both. Nevertheless, Rollins's career has not simply been uneven and controversial: in view of his prodigious gifts and oft-proven magnificence, the possibility exists that his potential has never been fully realised. If that is so, I am convinced that diffidence lies somewhere near the heart of the matter.

*****

I have never met Sonny Rollins, let alone interviewed him. I want therefore to reiterate that this book is a critical and discographical account of his career, not a biography in any true sense. I have tried throughout to place Rollins's work in as full a perspective as possible, in terms of both the development of jazz itself and wider cultural phenomena; that has led me to make certain inferences about his ambitions, motivation and musical nature. Those are always based on aural or written evidence, but they do not purport to be anything other than critical analysis.

My account is in four sections. Part One considers the musical and historical context in which Rollins emerged and then looks at his work from its beginnings up to his 1959 sabbatical. Part Two focuses on his 1960s come-back, while Part Three examines his re-appearance after a further lay-off and his work to the present day. And Part Four attempts a summary of the central characteristics of his style and musical concerns; this includes three transcriptions of Rollins solos by Ken Rattenbury

Notes

1 Donald L Maggin, *Stan Getz: A Life In Jazz* (New York: Morrow, 1996).

2 Quoted in Doug Ramsey's sleeve essay to the Verve Master Edition reissue of **Getz/Gilberto**, Verve 521 414-2.

3 *Ibid*

4 'One Sweet Letter', *Jazz Journal International*, ixl /12 (1996), 4.

5 *The Times*, July 14, 1997.

6 D.H.Lawrence, 'The Spirit Of Place', *Studies In Classic American Literature* (London: Penguin, 1970), 8.

7 **Focus** is on Verve 521 419-2 (Master Edition), **Sweet Rain** on Verve 815 054-2.

8 On Emarcy 838 770-2.

© Peter Symes

NEWK'S TIME: 1949-59

Many black people did feel that life would be better for them after World War II. There was a hopefulness expressed in (Bebop) whether it was conscious or not. It had joy, beauty and optimism.[1]

Ira Gitler

In terms of global history, the 1940s are chiefly famous for World War II. In terms of jazz history, the decade is mainly notable for Bebop – its germination, flowering and decline. The two events are closely connected.

There was a forward-looking energy about Bebop that matched the vigour of America's war effort; moreover, the euphoria occasioned by the war's triumphal end, and consonant dreams of a better world to be built, are reflected in Bebop's joyous momentum. Less happily, the United States's rapid decline into an ethos based on fear of the Soviet bloc and the consequent abandoning of most of those dreams can be paralleled with Bebop's transience as the commercial hub of American jazz. By the end of the decade America was involved in another war, in Korea; the harshness and disillusionment that conflict prompted can be seen as mirrored in the work of Miles Davis and others of his 'cool' persuasion. Their music, though based on Bebop, embodied a radical change of direction. America was already preparing itself, willingly, for what Gore Vidal has described as "the Golfer's dull terror"[2] – eight years of bland, arguably totalitarian conformism under the presidency of Dwight D. Eisenhower.

Even those whose interest in jazz falls somewhere between slight and zero probably know that the key figures of Bebop were Charlie Parker and Dizzy Gillespie. But it is important to bear in mind that, like all revolutions, Bebop did not 'simply happen'. Its seeds can be detected in several developments during the 1930s – developments which can be divided into general cultural matters and specifically musical ones.

In the former category, two important changes of attitude evolved. An increasing number of young black musicians viewed the white-dominated 'Swing' movement with distaste and resentment. Distaste because the vibrant guts of jazz had been domesticated and diluted in order that 'Swing' might attract a mass audience; resentment because that mass audience was drawn to white musicians whom the blacks regarded as third-rate or, worse, rip-off cynics. Of course, not all white bands were like that: those led by Artie Shaw and Benny Goodman were honest, exciting and innovative. Yet while many black musicians enjoyed and admired those outfits, their respect was nonetheless tinged with resentment: the huge success of Shaw and Goodman overshadowed the achievements of black orchestras, notably the now half-forgotten Chick Webb – "one of Harlem's great bands that should have got some of the plaudits that went to Goodman".[3]

Less angry but just as significant was a burgeoning and politically-focused Romanticism – a belief in jazz as a pioneering *art*. Those who espoused this credo saw themselves as fully self-conscious artists, as opposed to (mere) craftsmen-entertainers. That connoted a very different attitude to one's audience from the one exemplified by Louis Armstrong, some of whose showmanship was anathema to the new breed. Much though they still revered him as a musician, they disliked his populism, seeing it as perilously close to 'Uncle Tomming'.

Turning to specifically musical issues, more than a few leading practitioners had become increasingly tired of and frustrated by the limitations of 'Swing' and the jazz of the 30s. Their chief targets or causes for complaint were the lumpish rhythm sections, an over-reliance on tired chord sequences and the prevalence of execrable popular ditties as staple fare. Shaw and

Goodman showed a good deal of imagination in avoiding most of these traps; two musicians went further, not only transcending such limitations but in effect charting the Beboppers' path years in advance.

By the mid-30s Duke Ellington was a prolific and distinguished composer. His *penchant* for writing specifically for certain key musicians was an important gift, but it should not be allowed to obscure the rich density of his orchestral palette or the far-reaching subtlety of his harmonic awareness. It is no accident that arguably the finest incarnation of his Orchestra (the early 40s outfit now known as the Blanton-Webster band) assimilated the burgeoning idioms of bop with ease: in several respects Duke had been there already and for some time.

So had Art Tatum. His importance as an *influence* has often been overstated or simply misunderstood: such bewilderingly complete pianism did not so much influence pianists as inspire the kind of deep awe that forced all the sentient ones down a different path. And it wasn't just pianists he affected. Almost from the start, Tatum's astounding harmonic sophistication anticipated and even surpassed the eventual innovations of Bebop.

The separate but analogous prescience of the two men's music is adumbrated in Tatum's March 1933 recording of Ellington's *Sophisticated Lady*, one of four selections that comprised his first solo piano recording date.[4] Throughout Tatum respectfully preserves the wry elegance of Ellington's line; equally he recognises its immense harmonic possibilities, explored with a mature audacity that still takes the breath away. The incautious listener may find the dazzling runs merely decorative; in truth such apparent filigreeing amounts to nothing less than a total destructuring and re-assembly of the tune. That presaged what the Beboppers would do: take the chords of a well-known tune, reflect on their harmonic potential and thereby evolve a new melodic line, rechristening the result. The transmogrification of *How High The Moon* into *Ornithology* is perhaps the *locus classicus*.

There was a third crucial precursor of Bebop: the first 'Count' Basie Orchestra. Bill Basie on piano, bassist Walter Page, Freddie Greene on guitar and drummer Jo Jones revolutionised ideas of how a rhythm section might operate – how it should sound and what it could do. To suggest that Jones was *the* key figure might seem unwise, even foolish: all four were innovative masters of their craft, and like all top-class teams they were greater than the sum of their parts. Nevertheless, Jones's lightness of touch – which increased rather than compromised his swinging power – not only brought about the floating élan of the band as a whole: it perfectly complemented the work of tenor saxophonist Lester Young.

Young made his first recordings in Chicago on October 9, 1936, with Basie, Page and Jones, trumpeter Carl Smith and vocalist Jimmy Rushing. It was arguably the most electrifying debut in jazz history, and its impact – both immediate and far reaching – hinged on the fact that Young was the first tenorist not to sound like Coleman Hawkins, who had in effect 'invented' the tenor saxophone in the late 20s. Hawkins's sound was huge, his style swaggeringly masculine, and within a few years he had become the only role model. As Dave Gelly observes

> There was a majesty in Hawkins's playing, informed by a mind and an ear so comprehensive that the idea of anyone ever challenging him seemed laughable ... (his) grandeur was expressed through a tone not only broad but biting. It had what saxophonists call 'edge'.[5]

Young's tone had no edge at all. He floated rather than bit; his vibratoless, almost feminine sound seemed to imply phrases rather than state them, let alone chew them up in the Hawkinsesque way that characterised Young's tenor colleague (and alleged rival) in the Basie Orchestra, Herschel Evans.

Yet although Young's sound attracted all the initial attention, his rhythmic conception was even more significant, in that it came to influence jazz musicians of all kinds, not just saxophonists. Abetted by the similarly radical Jones, Young caressed the beat rather than drove it. The ferocity which his tone precluded was replaced by a gymnastic suppleness: he seemed to dance rather than stomp. But such insouciance and obliqueness were also deceptive: Young was as natural a swinger as jazz will ever see. He may not have had the obvious fire of Hawkins and Evans, but even at his most apparently casual he "really smoked", as Oscar Peterson once put it to me. His lithely fluent lines opened up a new territory: it wasn't 'better' than the previous one (whatever that might mean) but it was decidedly different, ushering in the seminal achievements of Parker and Gillespie.

Parker was one of the greatest geniuses of twentieth-century music. His very first recordings, made in Kansas City in 1937 but not issued until 1988,[6] reveal, despite comically awful sound, an already mature and complete style, and from the outset he was, it seems, incapable of playing less than sublimely, no matter what the (often highly unpropitious) circumstances. Poor material, inapposite accompanists, indifferent recording techniques, his personal condition – none of these appeared to matter: the music just poured out of him as from some divine stream.[7] His style was already pure Bebop when he arrived in New York City, a veteran of the Jay McShann and Earl Hines bands though still in his teens. And he at once influenced *everyone* – not just saxophonists but all horn players, pianists, bassists, guitarists, drummers, even singers. Nobody, not even Duke Ellington, has rivalled Parker in his scale of influence on jazz or the direct lessons musicians learnt from him.

Gillespie is usually held to be inferior to Parker, a judgement I consider inaccurate. It may be true that he lacked Parker's stupefying musical personality; it is certainly true that his influence as a player never matched that of his confrère. But there are good reasons for regarding Gillespie as the key figure of Bebop's history and lasting import. It was he above all others who codified and harnessed Bebop's revolutionary possibilities. For while Parker fronted some formidable groups, his gifts never included sound leadership or organisational acumen: he often had the greatest trouble just getting himself to a gig. Gillespie had, in addition to his own prodigious musical talent, a masterly grasp of public relations and of the business end of the jazz life. And it was he who formed what many regard as the most exciting jazz outfit ever, the only bona fide Bebop big band there has been. As vibraharpist Milt Jackson observed in a 1987 conversation with critic Charles Fox:

> In an ideal world, the United States Government would keep a big band permanently on hand for Dizzy to work with. People who've never seen Dizzy in front of a big band haven't really seen Dizzy at all.[8]

Between them Parker and Gillespie presided over a few precious years when Bebop was the central current of Jazz. That heyday can now be precisely located – 1945-48, culminating in the greatest recordings by the Gillespie Big Band, preceded by the only slightly less exciting exploits of Woody Herman's First Herd and many superb sessions featuring Parker and Bebop's young lions. It was a time of national euphoria. The war against fascism had been won; America had emerged not only as victor but as unambiguously the richest and most powerful nation on earth, and for a while that power was used with wisdom and beneficence. Major domestic programmes (most obviously the GI Bill) benefited both black and white; massive foreign aid was equally forthcoming, not just to her European allies but to defeated foes Germany and Japan as well. America had the money, the technology and, it appeared, the will to realise a vision of plenty and harmony.

A period of unparalleled domestic prosperity duly ensued.[9] But by 1948 America's bountiful attitudes had given way to something akin to global paranoia[10] and such reductive change was reflected in the nation's music. Less than two years after the exhilarating majesty of the Gillespie Big Band's *Manteca, Two*

Bass Hit and *Cubano Be, Cubano* Bop and Herman's *Caldonia, Your Father's Moustache* and *Blowin' Up A Storm,* Bebop had become commercial anathema in the USA (though it remained viable in Europe). For an all-too-brief time promoters, club owners, radio stations and record companies had clamoured and clambered for it; Gillespie had become a national figure; Bebop dominated national consciousness – even those who detested it, like Louis Armstrong, could not deny that it had broadened the idiom and ambit of jazz. Suddenly all that had changed. Within a few months Gillespie's big band had come to rely on singers to ensure bookings and air-time; by the turn of the decade Bebop appeared to be finished. Future years would in fact prove that as an art form and an essential idiom of jazz it was both durable and profoundly resourceful, but its time as a significantly popular phenomenon was over.

All the big bands suffered. Ellington was able to keep his going, but only by funding it through his song royalties. No other large aggregate survived intact, and Gillespie himself was forced to call it a day in mid-1949. Just how quickly Bebop died the commercial death is illustrated in Ira Gitler's story concerning leading Bebop trumpeter Red Rodney:

> His manager was a man named Ray Barron ... and he was on the phone in Prestige President Bob Weinstock's inner office, talking to a club owner in some small town in the Boston area. "I got this terrific bebop band for you," he began. "Click," went the other end of the line.[11]

Onto this turbulent and in many respects depressing stage strode Theodore Walter Rollins.

II

A lot of times jazz means no barriers

Sonny Rollins

There are three things that immediately establish Sonny Rollins as a singular jazz figure. First, his date of birth. It seems to be agreed that he celebrates his birthday on September 7; there is less unanimity about the *year* when he first saw the light of day. Anything from 1928 to 1931 has been put forward; if for now I have chosen to accept the one cited in Leonard Feather's *Encyclopedia of Jazz* – 1929 – the choice is arbitrary, for we all await definitive proof. His father was a career navy man who rose to the rank of Chief Petty Officer – about as high as a black could go in the Navy at that time. His mother was a native of the Virgin Islands; that West Indian heritage underscores a good deal of Rollins's art, especially his predilection for the calypso.

Second, Rollins was never – right up to his recording debut in 1948 – completely sure he wanted to be a musician. He had, and retains, considerable talent as a painter, and unlike virtually every other important musician of his era, Rollins does not appear to have had a visceral determination to carve out a career in jazz. That is not to suggest that his attitude to his craft has ever lacked seriousness: on the contrary, it connotes an independence of mind that has proved one of his most creative strengths. It does, however, imply a kind of diffidence that helps illuminate certain unusual features of his development.

Third, alone amongst the significant hornmen of his generation, Rollins had no experience of playing in a big band. (To this day his only recorded performances with a large jazz outfit are four tunes cut for Verve in 1958.) Parker and Gillespie, Getz, Zoot Sims, Dexter Gordon, Art Pepper, Sonny Stitt, 'Jug' Ammons, Lee Konitz, Gerry Mulligan, Eddie 'Lockjaw' Davis, Wardell Gray, Al Cohn – all these and many more spent their formative years in big bands, learning their craft within them. Big bands were the finest schools that have ever been available to jazz musicians; right up to the present time most jazzmen of note have at some time advanced or broadened their musical education in such a context. Rollins has never done this, and that alone makes him special.

Now, it would be absurd to suggest that Rollins has ever lacked craft. Naturally gifted, he was also highly conscientious from the start, always seeking to improve his knowledge of the saxophone and his mastery of it. But this process was largely effected alone. Not for him, as for Getz, Cohn and Sims, the symbiotic education of a 'Four Brothers' saxophone section. Rollins learnt through solitude, out of which grew an intense devotion to his instrument: Steve Lacy, a gifted reedman who has learnt much from Rollins, once remarked that he has "never seen anyone in love with the tenor saxophone the way Sonny is."[12] A characteristic both endearing and eloquent of the nature of Rollins's achievement, this perhaps accounts for his periodic, rather Garboesque desire to be alone. Most of the important lessons he has learnt musically he has learnt from himself and from his private passionate relationship with the saxophone.

Two matters already addressed may further explain why Rollins never spent any formative time in a big band. First, while it would be overstating the case to say he became a jazz musician by accident, there is a charmingly rough-and-ready quality to how he got started in the music business. Although he came from a musical family (a brother and sister both played instruments) he quickly became bored with early piano lessons, giving up at the age of ten, and in their place grew an ambition to draw. And second, by the time he became truly committed to music, the big bands were on the brink of folding and opportunities for young tyros were scarce indeed.

His renewed interest in music came about when a friend showed him a photo he had taken of himself and a saxophone. The instrument attracted Rollins and he decided to get one. Two more things spurred him on his way. He was fond of the music of Louis Jordan (of which more in a moment) and he happened to live in the same neighbourhood as Coleman Hawkins, whose music he liked anyway and whom he quickly came to hero-worship, hanging around just to get a glimpse of the great man. Even so, in the words of Joe Goldberg:

> Sonny still did not take music very seriously, and even today gives the impression of having fallen into the profession almost by chance.[13]

Rollins own account of his beginnings in jazz[14] suggests that his confidence as a musician had more to do with the realisation that Hawkins, Bud Powell and J.J.Johnson liked him personally than with a belief in his burgeoning artistry. The encouraging affection Rollins inferred from these men touched him deeply and can be seen as decisive in his choice of career.

Before looking at Rollins's first recordings, a further word about Louis Jordan is in order. Jordan had a highly successful career in the late 1930s and 40s with what has become known as a 'jump band'. Rollins has warmly remembered him as having "the first of the little blues bands, like Ray Charles has now."[15] Essentially a rhythm-&-blues outfit, Jordan's band offered high-class, impeccably precise and swinging 'good time music'. In 1945 he was the first to record *Caldonia*, which Woody Herman would soon turn into a Bebop classic; he was also the instigator of *Saturday Night Fish Fry* (a hit two decades later for Georgie Fame & Alan Price) and *Schooldays*, which became a staple part of Dizzy Gillespie's 1950s repertoire. What is fascinating – and crucial to any appraisal of Rollins's work – is that the Jordan influence is conspicuous both in its presence and its absence.

In a direct sense it explains Rollins's prediliction for the calypso and his many forays into musical forms as infectious as they are simple. But there is also much about his music that seems estranged from such an ethos. He may have drifted into the music business: once there he quickly became committed to the art of improvisation and, by extension, experiment. This resulted in many performances that, no matter what their many riches, can hardly be called serene or analogous to Jordan's 'good time music'. A great deal of Rollins's work is *difficult*. It is rewarding partly because of that, naturally: no enthusiast ever objects to being asked to do some work in the pursuit of pleasure and satisfaction. But I will say now that I find that Rollins's greatest achievements are those in which Jordan's spirit *is* present, and that such occasions are not as frequent as one might like them to have been.

Philip Larkin once defined the music of New Orleans as "synonymous with a particularly buoyant kind of jazz that seems to grow from a spontaneous enjoyment of living."[16] Those words can equally be applied to more than a few modernists – Oscar Peterson, Gillespie, the bands of Basie and Herman, Milt Jackson, Errol Garner and Rollins himself in Jordanesque mood. Such élan distinguishes the three performances I have asked Ken Rattenbury to transcribe – the 1956 *St. Thomas* from **Saxophone Colossus,** *I Know That You Know* from a 1957 date with Stitt and Gillespie, and *Three Little Words* from the 1965 **On Impulse!** That kind of joy amidst forbidding technical mastery also characterises every moment of the 1974 concert Rollins gave at Montreux, preserved on the album that provides my title, **The Cutting Edge.** Its five tracks abound with daring, ambition and a beauty both rhapsodic and vinegary, but above all else the evening captures him having an unreservedly good time. *Joie de vivre* and geniality just bubble out of him, qualities often missing in his allegedly more significant outings elsewhere. The Pleasure Principle lies at the heart of all his finest work.

* *

Sonny Rollins's first recordings first recordings were made with singer Babs Gonsalves in 1948.[17] So far as the tenorist's contribution is concerned, the music is for obsessive collectors only, since he is very much the ensemble player given no real chance to display his creativity. But such opportunities soon came. The word quickly went round about this likable New Yorker, and within a few months he was making his soloist's presence felt in precocious fashion.

J.J. Johnson used him on two dates in 1949. In February they cut four tracks, including Rollins's own composition *Audubon*, which Johnson not only used but bought. That itself was a compliment; the music also shows that, far from dutifully following his leader, Rollins was already capable of impressing the master-trombonist, especially in his muscular sense of time. He is not only completely at home with mature Bebop rhythms but intimates how to extend them structurally; moreover *Audubon* foreshadows the motific approach that would soon make Rollins a significant composer. Three months later Johnson took Rollins into the Prestige studios where another four tracks were recorded. This May session was completed by Kinny Dorham, John Lewis, Max Roach and bassist Leonard Gaskin, and featured another Rollins composition, *Hilo*, that further confirms his youthful mastery and rhythmic innovation.

A date made under Bud Powell's name in August 1949 is more impressive still. To play alongside master-boppers Powell, Fats Navarro, Tommy Potter and Roy Haynes amounted to a baptism of fire even fiercer than his sessions with Johnson, but Rollins was not in the least out-faced. On the various takes of *Dance of the Infidels*, *Wail* and *Bouncing with Bud* he not only embraces the art of improvisation with panache and audacity but in doing so breaks new ground.

The seminal importance of these performances hinges on two things, exemplified by the second take of *Bouncing with Bud*. First, Rollins plays 'against' Haynes's drums as well as feeding off them, creating a complexity absent even in Powell's brilliant outing. This points to an aspect of Rollins's playing that I don't believe has been critically dwelt on enough – his kinship with

Lester Young. As noted, 'Pres' was a rhythmic innovator of genius, even if his startling tone made some of his early audiences deaf to that fact. To hear the same kind of unerring virtuosity in a player whose attacking sound is so clearly founded on Hawkins is to be aware of an excitingly fertile synthesis. And like Young, Rollins "really smokes".

The second notable felicity is Rollins's precocious sense of structure. His solo impresses immediately – a series of long, essentially *legato* lines (another link with Young) delivered with satisfying raspingness; it is only later that one also becomes aware of the way in which he dismantles normal rhythmic conventions, treating his solo as an organic extended structure rather than as a succession of blowing choruses. It is this quality which inspired the ecstatic critical response to **Saxophone Colossus** seven years later; these 1949 tracks show it to have been a fundamental facet of Rollins's art from the beginning.

I do not think my opinion of Rollins's 1949 sides is hyperbolic; however, two things need to be said. First, several distinguished annotators of Rollins's career do not share that opinion; second, he was not thrust into the spotlight as a result of these recordings – unlike Stan Getz, whose teenage triumph on Woody Herman's *Summer Sequence* made him an international start almost overnight. To be sure, the *cognoscenti* quickly latched onto him; he worked with Art Blakey, Tadd Dameron and the never-recorded Chicago drummer, Ike Day, whom Rollins remembered as one of the finest musicians he ever encountered. But true fame was still some way off.

In 1951 he spent six months with Miles Davis. Nearly every stage of the trumpeter's career has caused controversy and debate, and this early one is no exception. One view is that at this time Davis's importance as a musician was out of all proportion to his technical skill. Though his tutelage was complete and he had starred on the momentous **Birth of the Cool**[18], his playing betrayed frequent fluffs or the kind of hesitant awkwardness that prompted one critic to compare his approach to that of a man walking on egg-shells. A contrary opinion is that the fluffs were, if not deliberate, the natural result of a musician looking to extend his emotional vocabulary and that, like the otherwise very different Roy Eldridge, Davis was driven rather than maladroit.

Each case can be supported by judicious discographical selection: those who take the more complimentary view cite in particular a 1949 Paris concert where Davis is in blistering form. The real point to make here is that Rollins's time with Davis was an enjoyably enabling one. Their recordings find him honing his tone and adventurous harmonic sense while feeding off the young trumpeter's angular thoughtfulness, and once again the tenorist's precocious authority is notable. On such cuts as *Whispering* (January 1951) and *It's Only a Paper Moon* (October) one could be forgiven for thinking that it is he, not Davis, who is the senior player, despite the trumpeter's trenchant swing and characteristically memorable phrasing.

Whether or not Davis was still short of technical mastery as a player, he had a number of other qualities that explained his success and status. He was always a willing pupil; he also had an iron will and great courage: it took guts and a determination at once humble and self-assured to struggle through all those initial dates with Parker and other virtuosi. Moreover, he had an unusually perceptive musical brain, and was a superb judge of other musicians and of how best to work with and off them. To work with Davis invariably led to mutual nourishment and growth. Rollins, however lacked Davis's confidence, and while their partnership was indeed productive, a fair amount of the tenorist's time was spent studying and re-thinking his playing. Even though he did not withdraw from the music scene altogether, it is legitimate to identify these months as the first of his 'woodshedding' periods.[19]

The desire to study and the conviction that one can always improve are laudable qualities. Nevertheless, Rollins's *penchant* for withdrawal has another side – in no sense reprehensible but indicative of a strange uncertainty. In 1951, aged just twenty-two, he had made at the very least an auspicious start. He was a mature technician and a convincing soloist; he had a fertile imagination and considerable talent as a composer; he swung hard and instinctively; moreover, his rhythmic perception was such that some already regarded him as a leading force in jazz. Given all that, it is odd that he should have needed to 're-think'. The most obvious and natural thing to do would be to discover more by playing, by broadening his 'road' experience, his awareness of other musicians and of the full implications of what he had already achieved. (Exactly the course that Davis had followed, in fact.) Young, strong and in demand, he chose to spend a good deal of time away from the bandstand and external musical stimuli. Why?

There seem to me to be four main reasons. First, he was already undergoing what are euphemistically termed 'personal problems' – i.e. drug abuse. He was hardly alone in this; nor was he unique in becoming hooked because of his passionate desire to emulate Charlie Parker in as many ways as possible. Drummer Don Lamond has summed it up well:

> You know how kids are. Everything their idols did was right. So the kids did it too.[20]

Maybe twenty-two years old is rather more senior than anything connoted by "kid", but the principle holds. It would take Parker's own disapproval of Rollins's habit and the clean-living example set by his eventual front-line partner Clifford Brown to wean Rollins off drugs, and although he escaped the terminal addiction that has tragically littered so much jazz history, it need hardly be said that the effects of his habit were distortive and debilitating. Parker was remarkable in that he could play like an angel while juiced to the eyebrows; few were so self-destructively gifted or had the musical confidence to ignore any and all physical shortcomings while playing. Rollins certainly hadn't. He had never been completely sure he wanted to be a professional musician until it actually happened; his frequent drug-haze can scarcely have increased his sense of commitment to the working musician's life.

Second, it is reasonable to assume that Rollins – a gentle, self-effacing man – felt under considerable pressure by now. He knew that he had extended Parker's gospel in an important way, and it is no easy thing to be in the front line when young, inexperienced and not entirely sure about what one wants to do with one's life and music. For all the majesty of his playing, Rollins's personality tends to the contemplative and introverted: he does not relish the spotlight except on those (comparatively rare) occasions when he is at one with himself and his work.

Third, the year in question was a far from happy time in America in general and jazz in particular. Post-war euphoria had vanished; the Korean war had alone crushed most of that mid-40s hope, and the gloom was deepened by such tawdry episodes as the prosecution of Alger Hiss.[21] The McCarthy witch-hunts were only a few months away; a sense of decline into fear and awkwardness was palpable. Most germane in Rollins's case was the evident stagnation (if not actual regression) of Civil Rights and the overall lot of America's blacks. Rollins has never been a vociferous supporter of Black Power and the like, but his reflective nature has a fierce core of idealism and racial awareness. Indeed, in an interview with Ira Gitler he articulated as moving a summary of jazz as I know:

> Jazz was not just a music: it was a social force in this country, and it was talking about freedom and people enjoying things for what they are and not having to worry about whether they were supposed to be black, white and all that stuff. Jazz has always been a music that had that kind of spirit. Now I believe that for that reason the people who *could* push jazz have *not* pushed jazz, because that's what jazz means. A lot of times, jazz means no barriers.[22]

It is not hard to see in those words the beliefs that would inspire one of Rollins's finest achievements, the 1958 **Freedom Suite**. More immediately, they are eloquent of the egalitarian joy that characterised his formative musical years, the collapse of which produced a different musical climate that the tenorist did not find wholly congenial.

Fourth, a case can be made for Rollins as 'a sprinter', one who works best in shortish bursts. That is contentious on two counts: it ignores the fact that Rollins has been a major jazz star for fifty years and it seems to fly in the face of his remarkable stamina in performance. The latter quality is not consistent: Rollins is one of the very few musicians who can play like a nervous dog one night and produce sublime jazz for four hours the next. Ronnie Scott's recollection is illuminating:

> We did a tour with (Sonny), same rhythm section. I'd play for half an hour, then introduce him, and he'd play the rest of the concert. We did one at Liverpool University, and he was in one of his strange moods. And he just never played anything. He'd start a snatch of something, and the guys would catch on and start to play; as soon as they did, he's drift off into something else – fragments. And really after half an hour it just got boring – very weird. People slow-handclapped, walked out, all sorts of things. Eventually he said "Play with me," so the two of us had to kind of play something more or less understandable, because there were two of us. But the next night in Manchester, it was *incredible*, absolutely incredible. About the best music I've ever heard.[23]

When he is 'on', Rollins's energy and endurance take the breath away. Ours, that is, not his: at such times he seems capable of playing for ever.

Nonetheless, I stick to that 'sprinter' remark. In the course of preparing this book, I made out a list of Rollins's records from 1949 to the present: their 'grouping' is very interesting. He recorded nothing in 1952 or for nearly all of 1955; he had two full years' woodshedding from 1959 to 1961; he seems to have played little and recorded virtually nothing between 1967 and 1972; and although since then he has worked more or less regularly be can still go for a considerable time without recording. Studying that overall pattern leads me to deduce that Rollins is a fast-fuse operator, one who works in high-voltage 'charges' rather than in a more relaxed, less dramatic rhythm.

Indeed, that most famous period of withdrawal (59-61) was perhaps due in part to the biggest spurt of creative energy in his entire career. In just two-and-a-half years, beginning with a clutch of dates made with the Brown-Roach band in 1956 and ending with a jam session for Contemporary in October 1958, Rollins made over two dozen records. All of them are extremely good; over half of them can safely be called classics. And I would argue that such a 'burst' meant that Rollins simply needed a rest. His career both before and since those golden thirty months indicates that he does not find it natural to perform week in, week out; he plays to a different drummer from most men of his stature, and the partial withdrawal during 1951-2 offers the first evidence of this key facet of his musical personality.

Rollins's personal life was undergoing considerable and not entirely fruitful changes at this time, which might further explain his need for semi-withdrawal. But recorded evidence – specifically **Sonny Rollins and the Modern Jazz Quartet** – does not point to any consequent musical changes. Though high in quality, the album is something of a hotch-potch, misleadingly headlined: only four of the thirteen sides feature the titular musicians in a session which did not take place until October 1953. Of the remaining nine tracks, eight date from December 1951 and *I Know*, with thoughtful piano from one Miles Davis, was cut eleven months before that.

The MJQ tracks are very successful, with Rollins's angular lines fluent and swinging, offset by John Lewis's stealthy power and Milt Jackson's quicksilver blues-soaked silkiness. However, the music does not evince any noticeable development from what is to be found elsewhere on the album. The late Martin Williams rates *Mambo Bounce* very highly;[24] while sharing his admiration, I cannot go along with his further contention that it constitutes something of a breakthrough for the tenorist. The mambo form is nudged rather than explored: the tune is in essence an extrovert stomping blues that showcases Rollins's harmonic sophistication as satisfyingly as his intrinsic swing. All well and good, indeed splendid; however, *Newk's Fadeaway* is an equally impressive essay in the art of hard bop,[25] and the aforementioned *I Know* is similarly fleet and cogent. In sum, I would argue that Rollins was already a mature exponent of hard bop by January 1951 and simply consolidated his excellence over the next two years – a view cemented by the justly celebrated session recorded on January 30, 1953 which forms one side of the Esquire LP **Collector's Item** (not yet issued on CD).

The personnel is mightily impressive: leading bop pianist Walter Bishop, bassist Percy Heath and drummer Philly Joe Jones underpin a frontline of Rollins, Miles Davis and Charlie Parker (billed as 'Charlie Chan' for contractual reasons). Nobody plays less than well, although amidst his flashing expertise Parker does not always sound fully at home with the alto's big brother; in my judgment, however, Rollins is the star of the date, his work consistently the most vibrant and acute. One regrets his absence on *'Round Midnight*, especially when that is followed by the session's highspot, the superb *Compulsion*. In all **Collector's Item** is one of the essential Rollins records, and seemingly a most auspicious one.

In fact, the next two years were somewhat chequered. Musically he continued to develop, working in a wide range of contexts. The aforementioned date with the MJQ took place in October 1953; June 29 of the following year saw a reunion with Miles Davis in the company of Horace Silver and Milt Jackson that comprises most of **Bags' Groove**, made under the trumpeter's name. Everyone plays splendidly, but the date is chiefly notable for the inclusion of three Rollins compositions that have become modern jazz standards – *Oleo, Doxy* and *Airegin*. The last is particularly important in that in characteristically oblique fashion (the title is Nigeria spelt backwards) it signals Rollins's deep interest in the African roots of jazz and his quietly profound racial awareness. *Oleo* went on to become a staple part of Davis's repertoire while *Doxy* has proved as supple as durable (Rollins cut a superb version five years later with John Lewis). One wonders just what the compilers of the *Penguin Guide to Jazz on CD, LP & Cassette* were about when they opined "Rollins hasn't shown much interest in composition."[26]

In August 1954 Rollins recorded **Moving Out** with Art Blakey, the Powell-like Elmo Hope and the trumpeter who would prove a stalwart partner on many future occasions, Kinny Dorham. All four sides abound in good things: the tenorist is especially cogent on *Solid* (towards the end a figure appears that is reincarnated over ten years later in the final bars of **On Impulse!**'s *Blue Room*) and intensely lyrical on the deceptively simple *Silk 'N' Satin*.

The fall of 1954 saw his first collaboration with that quirky and enormously influential genius, Thelonious Monk, whose angular style and radical harmonic approach proved an ideal foil for him. The session originally known as **Work**, made under the pianist's name, was, though musically excellent, another Prestige rag-bag: two trio tracks, a quintet version (fronted by Rollins and French hornist Julius Watkins) of Monk's remarkable *Friday The 13th*, and two, *The Way You Look Tonight* and *I Want To Be Happy* by a Watkins-less quartet. These five sides are on CD as **Thelonious Monk & Sonny Rollins**; and third quartet performance made on the same day is – rather perversely – included on **Moving Out**.

Rollins is excellent throughout. I cannot agree with Ronald Atkins that he is "hesitant" on *Friday The 13th* or that he is "enmeshed within the piece's ever-recurring patterns":[27] he is incisively at home with this challenging composition, and the performance's only flaw is Watkins's somewhat lumbering solo. Philp Larkin was much nearer the mark in February 1968 when (surprisingly to some) he nominated the reissued Work as his Record of the Month:

> For narrowness of repertoire and sameness of treatment Monk beats Kid Ory by several miles, but these five tracks are full of snap, crackly and even pop, with a prelapserian Sonny Rollins tearing into *The Way You Look Tonight* and *I Want To Be Happy* in a manner ... gay, fruitful, and energetic ... This (music) is far from the killer-diller tradition, but so original that it compels attention.[28]

Yet these fine records do not tell the whole story. By now Rollins was a confirmed drug addict, and his career began to resemble a firework display held in pouring rain – occasionally dazzling, more often spluttering fitfully. Despite his success and rapidly growing reputation he was frustrated, and perhaps fearing that he had reached some sort of dead end, he took most of the next year off. This second period of woodshedding was a success: though still in the grip of addiction he emerged refreshed rather than enervated, full of renewed confidence. An indeed, in many respects 1956 proved an *annus mirabilis* for Rollins. His career blossomed via several outstanding recordings; even more important, tenorist Harold Land left the prestigious Clifford Brown-Max Roach Quintet and Rollins was asked to replace him. It was a move that set up the most important influence of his musical and personal life.

III

When they said Clifford Brown had been killed in an auto accident, God it was hard to believe. I just crumpled inside and began to cry. Then I thought to myself, is it possible to write a melody that would indicate the way he used to play? ... (Finally) I decided it was as good as I could get it. I called it "I Remember Clifford". I played it to Dizzy on the piano, and he said, "Gee, that's beautiful." I hope in some way the song will stop people forgetting the great, the immortal Clifford Brown. He was the only man I ever cried about. And he was worth crying over.

Benny Golson[29]

Jazz abounds in sad stories, but few can be sadder than what happened to 'Brownie'. Many of the personal tragedies that so populate jazz history contain an element of self-destruction: Parker, Billie Holiday, Lee Morgan and Lester Young come most immediately to kind. But everyone who knew Brown seems to agree that he was not only a wonderful musician but a wholly admirable man – mature, kind, self-possessed in the best sense, humorous and both sensitive and tough. Sonny Rollins himself has observed:

> Clifford was so together as a person you wouldn't have believed it. For a guy that plays that much to be so humble and beautiful, it was just amazing. So I tried to be nice after that.[30]

It was Brown's character and personal example that made a crucial difference to Rollins's drug problem, successfully hardening his determination to get 'clean'. But Brown's influence was profound in less dramatic ways. He was a bubbling extrovert with a merry wit – a stark contrast to the rather lugubrious Rollins of the time. When Rollins began to tire of his nick-name 'Newk' – he bore a strong facial resemblance to baseball star Don Newcombe – Brown gnomically started to call him Rowntree instead. Eventually Rollins felt himself forced to ask why, and got the reply:

> Well, you look like a boxer I used to know. They called him Rowntree. Reason they called him that was he always used to get knocked out in Round Three.

Rollins loved Brown, not least for that joyous, unmalicious humour: that love still shines from the recordings they made. Not that they weren't competitive: on the contrary, the audacious fashion in which they challenge and feed off each other is perhaps the most striking characteristic of their work together.

But then, loving confrontation is in a sense the lifeblood of jazz and it is something that Rollins has perhaps not had enough of during his lengthy career. One could argue about that; what is beyond argument is that the Brown-Roach sides are unique in Rollins's *oeuvre* – the only time when he worked regularly with a frontline partner who was not only his equal but arguably his superior.[31] For almost eight months he thrived on this on-the-road symbiosis, and it is not melodramatic to suggest that Brown's death in June was a long-term tragedy for Rollins as well as a ghastly loss to jazz as a whole.

Fortunately a large number of recordings preserve the group's work, both live and in the studio. Particularly rewarding are the four cuts on Brown's **The Quintet Vol. 2** (Emarcy) and the prestige albums **Sonny Rollins and Clifford Brown** and **Sonny Rollins Plus Four**, which was Brown's last record date. On all performances the horns complement each other perfectly, Brown's golden tone offset by the vinegary but full tones of the tenorist. Their rhythmic mastery is especially noteworthy. Driven by the mighty Roach and hardly less well served by Richie Powell's piano, Brown and Rollins consistently achieve immense power without compromising their equal commitment to melody and form.

As with all the finest jazz there is throughout a sublime feeling of untapped resources even when heat is at its fiercest – a quality that distinguishes **Sonny Rollins Plus Four** in particular. Potentially frenetic cuts such as *Kiss and Run* and *I Feel a Song Coming On* are instead elevated into classics of hard bop, joyously empathetic and masterly in structure. The album also offers further evidence of Rollins's compositional powers. Brown revels in both *Valse Hot* and *Pent-Up House*, as does the composer himself: superficially diverse, they have a penetrating boldness that confirms the latent presaged by *Audubon* and *Hilo*. Best of all, Rollins is imbued with a confidence that had seemed absent only a year before. That new assurance informs the delicious *Count Your Blessings*, where Brown does not play, allowing its two-and-a-half minutes to be a showcase for Rollins at his most incisive.

All the Brown-Rollins-Roach recordings are important. This was one of *the* great jazz combos, and one can only speculate mournfully on what further heights it might have scaled had fate been kinder. Brown and Roach were masters who would have emerged as stars whatever their context; Powell and bassist George Morrow remain two of the most under-lionised sidemen in jazz history. Rollins was the 'X Factor'. The Quintet with Harold Land had, goodness knows, been fine enough: Land's playing was supple and melodious and his partnership with Brown occasioned many riches. But Rollins brought to the group's work an increased rhythmic intensity and adventurous feeling for form. That excellent young trumpeter Nicholas Payton (on whom Brown was a profound early influence) offered these telling remarks in October 1997:

> Harold Land is great, don't get me wrong ... but I think playing alongside Sonny intensifies Clifford's musicianship. Rhythmically and harmonically, he is a lot more developed than on (his) earlier recordings. Sonny is like Clifford on sax, and those two together just take the music to another level. [32]

If Rollins made a crucial difference to Brown, the converse was equally true. Away from the Quintet Rollins cut two albums for Prestige that show why he was now regarded as the most influential tenorist around. **Work Time** is a classy quartet date with Morrow, Roach and the pianist who would illuminate many future Rollins sessions, Ray Bryant. Outstanding anyway and a pioneering example of the tenorist's fondness for 'odd-ball' material,* *There's No Business Like Show Business* is explored with exhilarating rigour at an express tempo; the abrupt ending is inspired. *There Are Such Things* is rhapsodic and inquisitive at once, and again the ending – suspended this time – is perfect. As Ira Gitler shrewdly observes, "There is an essence of Hawkins in this ballad without it sounding like him."[33]

In May 1956 came **Tenor Madness.** Such a beautiful and fascinating record deserved a less silly title: there is nothing "mad" about this music, in the sense of either "angry" or "uncontrolled". Four of the five cuts team Rollins with Miles Davis's then rhythm section, Red Garland, Paul Chambers and Philly Joe Jones, and their empathy is remarkable. *When Your Lover Is Gone* is both enchanting and trenchant, and *My Reverie* – a song Rollins would return to nearly twenty years later (on **Nucleus**) – is silkily delightful and about as mad as a chocolate soufflé.[34] There's a sublimely relaxed feel to all these sides that gives an added dimension to their tender passion and melodic exploration: the music is, in a word, lovely.

Rightly or wrongly, however, the album remains chiefly famous for its title track, which adds the tenor John Coltrane. A driving blues bearing a very strong resemblance to Parker's *Now's The Time*, *Tenor Madness* has been seen by many as a 'tenor battle' similar to Wardell Gray and Dexter Gordon's *The Hunt, The Chase* and *The Steeplechase* or the kind of jousting that Norman Granz encouraged in his Jazz At The Philharmonic concerts. I find this view simplistic – the music is, for all its fire,

* I examine this facet of Rollins's art in Part Four.

too thoughtful and sophisticated to warrant such labelling. But if one insists on seeing it as primarily a confrontation,[35] Rollins is comfortably the winner – and I use the adverb advisedly. He exudes assurance and control; his tone is warmer and much broader emotionally than Coltrane's and he is rhythmically more relaxed and varied: he plays with a controlled swagger that makes his partner's lines frenetic in comparison. That is not to denigrate Coltrane – his work is full of probing invention and he also swings ferociously (a facility he was sadly to abandon in his last years) – but properly to celebrate Rollins's structural mastery and humorous, affirmative virtuosity. Both with and away from the Brown-Roach Quintet Rollins seemed to have entered a period of pure serendipity where everything was going right.

Such a sense of blessed fortune came to a hideously abrupt end on June 25, 1956 on the Pennsylvania Turnpike, in a crash which claimed the lives of Brown, Powell and the pianist's wife Nancy; Rollins was in the car travelling behind. The jazz world was appalled by Brown's death; to dwell on how Rollins felt would be obtrusive even now. The issue can, however, be approached via an analogous tale.

Sir Garfield Sobers is arguably the greatest cricketer who has ever lived. He was the lucky survivor of a car crash which claimed the life of a close colleague who was also a loved friend. In 1959 Sobers was at the wheel of a car which crashed on its way to London, injuring West Indian fast bowler Tom Dewdney and killing Collie Smith, a cricketer hardly less gifted than Sobers himself, who was unhurt. Once the immediate aftermath of grief had passed, Sobers brought to his cricket a new determination and a new dimension of genius. Maybe he was driven by a kind of guilt – not because he was at fault in the crash (he wasn't) but simply because of his own luck therein; in any event, for all that he remained a dazzling entertainer, his game evinced a greater responsibility and degree of steel. Not for nothing, Trevor Bailey has argued, did Sobers reserve some of his greatest exploits for Sabina Park, Kingston: Collie Smith was a Jamaican.[36]

Sonny Rollins showed a similar resolve and aesthetic advance following Brown's death: the next two years would see what some think is still the apex of his career. However, although the analogy with Sobers is I hope telling, it contains a flaw: the finest album produced in this period – indeed, to my mind his greatest ever – was cut four days *before* Brown's death. Those with a taste for the spooky might deduce that Brown's last gift was thus to inspire the man who had gained so much from him.

Anyone approaching **Saxophone Colossus** in the late 1990s with critical analysis in mind has a daunting task. Few albums have been the subject of such extensive commentary: Gunther Schuller's structural appreciation of *Blue Seven* is as famous as masterly, Martin Williams and Joe Goldberg are no less cogent, and between them they say much that cannot be improved upon.[37] However, I start with one mildly contentious opinion. Although all five tracks are magnificent, I would argue that the brightest jewel – and the album's most important track – is not *Blue Seven*, but *St. Thomas*. The former is undoubtedly a masterpiece, but James Lincoln Collier is persuasive when he observes

> It seems to me that far too much was made of (*Blue Seven*). It is true that on it Rollins return over and over again to a basic figure taken from a simple theme. He had done this before; for example, on *St Thomas*... or... on *Vierd Blues*, made a couple of years earlier with Davis. But this was hardly an innovation. Oliver's famous *Dippermouth Blues* solo is built round two figures, which keep returning in different forms; Armstrong builds the up-tempo section of *Muggles* out of variations on a skeletal figure; and Davis, too, liked to play with simple figures.[38]

In one respect this is less than fair to Rollins, whose combination of the sophisticated harmonics of Bebop and his own formal elegance is quite different from features of the earlier jazz cited and more penetrating than any of Davis's structural innovations. But Collier is surely right to suggest that *Blue Seven* is not unique in Rollins's career up to that point. *St. Thomas* does all the things that have been claimed for its stable-mate, and it does them in a performance which is additionally a definitive essay in the art of swinging. There is a bounce and extrovert snap to *St. Thomas* that celebrate the bedrock of jazz and its unique contribution to music. Moreover, although Max Roach is mordantly brilliant on *Blue Seven*, his drumming does not thrill in the way it does on *St. Thomas*, where his solo is as much a structural masterpiece as Rollins's. And his work beneath the tenorist is breathtaking in its sensual fire and rhythmic empathy: the two men play as if they were extensions of each other.

Mention must also be made of Rollins's peerless reading of the ballad *You Don't Know What Love Is*, with its marvellous final cadenza and the extrovert *Strode Rode*, a track I become ever more fond of and which deserves better than its consensual 'third place' to the two more celebrated sides. A Rollins composition, *Strode Rode* is a majestic blues – the form that had from the start inspired his most audaciously inventive improvising and which would dominate his work for the rest of the decade. Rollins's rolling legato lines here are his hottest playing on the date, climaxed by a succession of stop-choruses which are a distillation of pure virility. There is no more exciting sound than Rollins at his most ferociously joyful: not the least feature of this album's greatness is the generous scope afforded that central quality.

In sum, **Saxophone Colossus** deserves its fame both as a work of art and as a pivotal moment in Rollins's career. On the one hand it was a culmination of his activity so far, climactic proof of how productive had been his time with Brown; on the other it looked forward to a quite extraordinary spell of wide-ranging creativity.

The first instance was **Rollins Plays for Bird**, whose highspot is the twenty-seven minute medley that opens it. Joined once more by Kinny Dorham and backed by pianist Wade Legge, Morrow and Roach, Rollins fashions the seven tunes into both a tribute to Parker's art and a notable extension of it. *I Remember You*, complete with wittily apposite quotations from *Someday I'll Find You* and *They Can't Take That Away From Me* are especially fine Rollins vehicles; Dorham shines on *My Melancholy Baby* and *Just Friends* and Legge deals expertly with *Old Folks*. What I like most about this ambitious enterprise is its mellowness: the expected bite and rhythmic virtuosity are there too, but there's also a decidedly genial quality to everyone's playing, Rollins's in particular.

This is all the more remarkable in view of the state of his personal life at the time. By now he was off drugs, but Brown's death was of course a dreadful blow, and in all Sonny was far from "together", as Joe Goldberg reveals:

> Several pressures were operating on Rollins at this. He was married, as he puts it, "promiscuously". It did not work out. "I just wanted to get married," he says, "so I looked around, and found somebody, and I did." "Promiscuous" is also the work he uses to describe his recording activities. He wanted and needed money, and recording was the quickest way to get it, so he recorded for anyone and everyone who ask him ...Some idea of his promiscuity can be gotten by a listing of labels: Riverside, Atlantic, Blue Note, Period, Verve, Contemporary – all soon had Rollins records. Sonny was for hire, and almost everyone was interested.[39]

By rights, maybe, such whoring after record companies ought to have made his work a succession of tawdry pot-boilers in which art was cynically sacrificed to money-lust. Nothing could be further from the truth. Rollins may have been a capricious, confused, "promiscuous" man: he was also a great artist. He had an enormous amount to say and full confidence now in when and how to say it, and for over two years his work gloriously transcended day-to-day problems.[40]

December 1956 found Rollins in three different studios recording **Tour de Force** (Prestige), **Volume One** (Blue Note) and a further collaboration with Monk on the pianist's **Brilliant Corners** (Riverside). All are top-class: the material is as varied as are the musicians, but Rollins's inventiveness and flexibility are prodigious. Hardly less notable is his continued compositional prowess: of the ten tracks which made up the Prestige and Blue Note sessions, seven of the tunes are his. On **Tour de Force** *Ee-ah* is a commanding series of blues variations rooted in a three-note figure, while *B.Swift* and *B. Quick* (based respectively on *Cherokee* and *Lover*) are ferociously powerful. And if his writing on **Volume One** is less memorable, his playing certainly isn't: partnered by trumpeter Donald Byrd and assisted by that wonderful pianist Wynton Kelly, his debut as leader for the label is a triumph, more than fulfilling the rich promise of those first Blue Note sides with Bud Powell.

Those three albums completed a twelve-month period that began with **Work Time** which the *Penguin Guide to Jazz on CD, LP & Cassette* rightly calls "an astounding year on record."[41] 1957 was no less fruitful. He was (somewhat belatedly, it appears now) voted 'New Star' by *Down Beat*'s critics in the 1957 poll, and his work was as absorbing as ever. By now Rollins was becoming as renowned for his cryptic humour – especially his prediliction for 'weird' material – as for the quality and variety of his enterprise. As a result he particularly appealed to those who concurred with Whitney Balliett's famous* definition of jazz as "the sound of surprise".[42] It seemed that all one could predict about a new Rollins record was that (a) it would be excellent and (b) there was a good chance it would confound all expectation. That was duly the case with his first 1957 album, recorded in Los Angeles and aptly entitled **Way Out West**[43].

It was his first excursion into the pianoless group. He had wanted to try this format for some time, and as Lester Koenig revealed on the original LP essay:

* And wholly inadequate. I look to justify that remark in Part Four.

> The desire was reinforced by the fact that Ray Brown was in Los Angeles with the Oscar Peterson Trio, and Shelly Manne was also in town with his own group. If you had contemplated playing with only bass and drums, you would be hard put to find two better men than Brown and Manne, each an acknowledged master of his instrument ...[44]

Undoubtedly true; yet Koenig's encomium dramatises the date's second apparently remarkable feature. Rollins working with *Oscar Peterson's* bassist and a drummer who amongst all else was closely associated with *André Previn*? Whatever next?

The question may seem frivolous, but answering it in fact provides valuable opportunity to reflect on Rollins's true musical nature and what he had done so far. His original model was Coleman Hawkins; from the outset the seminal influence of Lester Young was equally evident. Those pre-bop Titans continued to inform the core of his playing, for all that he of course also responded to Parker's innovations and indeed extended them.[45] It is therefore no surprise that Rollins should choose Brown and Manne: all three were coming through the same door. Not only had Brown been a member of the historic Gillespie Big Band, to which bebop and hard bop owed so much: he had also been the original bassist in the group that was later christened The Modern Jazz Quartet. Rollins had already recorded successfully with the MJQ and would soon do so again. Furthermore, Oscar Peterson was as much a child of bop as Rollins, though like him his influences came from earlier times. The on-the-road repertoire of the 1957 Peterson Trio was just as venturesome and broad in its own way as Rollins's was, and although a head-to head meeting between tenorist and pianist was admittedly never very likely, their roots and achievements were and are a lot more analogous than the casual (or lazy) listener might think. And as Koenig pointed out, Brown and Manne were masters of their craft whom Rollins really wanted: as reliable as open to adventure[46], they were ideal.

I stress all that not simply out of irritation at narrow-minded categorisation of musicians and styles. That is always tiresome, but in some cases it is more reasonable than in others. The overriding point is that Rollins's playing was *always* a mixture of the traditional and the radical. All the work discussed so far re-affirms the bedrock values of mainstream jazz as much as it explores exciting new directions. During 1957 Rollins not only continued to celebrate both 'sides' of his work and musical nature: on record it seemed at times as if he was highlighting them alternately.

The pianoless music of **Way Out West** is a great success. Thanks to Brown's huge sound and agile virtuosity there is no loss of harmonic density, and Manne's versatility and sheer drive ensure there is no loss of percussive attach either. In addition, the format affords Rollins the kind of freedom to anticipate or even substitute harmony – a quality evident in his work before but never so pronounced. **Way Out West** is remarkable in other ways too. The material is an extraordinary mélange even by the tenorist's standards – a couple of Rollins originals; the Isham Jones standard *There Is No Greater Love;* that great rarity in the tenorist's recorded *œuvre,* an Ellington song (*Solitude*); and the two tunes that most reflect the album's title, *I'm An Old Cowhand* and *Wagon Wheels*. Such material might seem only good for a giggle, but it works triumphantly. The former builds up a prodigious head of steam, and while it is full of humour the wit is always affectionate, even admiring; the same goes for the treatment of *Wagon Wheels*, which lopes along with deceptive charm until the switch to a driving four-four beat. Amongst all else, this exemplifies the album's exquisite wit: nothing could be less 'way out' than Rollins's stirring playing if one has in mind what the term then signified in jazz *argot*, "extreme and/or ostentatiously unconventional". The grandeur of *Wagon Wheels* is both immediately accessible and appropriate to the pioneering spirit that **Way Out West** enshrines.

Lest that last remark seem simplisticly referential, it should be stressed that Rollins wanted the album to celebrate not only the spirit of the West but specifically the *black* West. In an interview with the tenorist published in 1995, Michael Jarrett suggest that "Jazz is metaphorically associated with the myths of the American West; the musician as outlaw-hero; the music as a movement or a push forward," to which Rollins replied:

> That's right. I've never thought of it in those words, but that's quite true. When I was a boy, I had seen all those all-black films. There was a fellow who used to sing in Duke Ellington's band, Herb Jeffries. He was in an all-black Western ...That made an impression on me. And of course, as we all know, there were black cowboys. All of these things were in my mind.[47]

Jarrett's piece reveals two other things of interest. First, photographer William Claxton's appropriation of the iconography of the American West for the album's cover was Rollins' idea – "I thought the whole thing was really right."[48] Superficially outrageous and enduringly witty, the cover sought to complement the music in a fundamental and organic way. Second, seeing that cover made a young Englishman decide he wanted to be a musician – strikingly analogous to Rollins's own inspiration on seeing the photography of a friend with a saxophone.[49] The Englishman's name was Courtney Pine.

Although it will be evident that **Way Out West** is a favourite of mine, I would not necessarily cite it as amongst Rollins's best; that said, it has several claims to be counted amongst his most fascinating, and it was certainly influential.[50] And the session illuminated one more facet of Rollins's art, as Lester Koenig observed:

> When he produced the sheet music for *There Is No Greater Love*, he read the words to Ray and Shelly and explained that while blowing he liked to think of the words and whey they

> meant. "It helps me," he said. And so *No Greater Love* becomes more than just a pretty ballad; even Sonny's tone becomes fuller and warmer, and the performance communicates on a highly emotional level.[51]

Another link in a particularly important chain: the kind of dedicated verbal awareness that enriches phrasing and grasp of mood is most famously associated with Lester Young.

Two weeks later Rollins and Max Roach cut **Jazz In 3/4 Time,** an invigorating programme of waltzes that consolidated the experiments with time that had been launched by *Valse Hot* on **Sonny Rollins Plus Four.** They also recorded three pieces not in waltz time, including a furiously satisfying *It Don't Mean A Thing* and the superb *Love Letters*, whose inspired arrangement I take to be Roach's work. Rollins starts things off at his most ravishing; a beautifully judged change of tempo ushers in Kinny Dorham's puckishly tender solo before pianist Bill Wallace restores the original mood with a brief but impressive ballad interlude. Finally an up-tempo Rollins takes over commandingly before the exquisite ending. These tracks, along with six others recorded in September 1956 (including a magnificent *Body and Soul*), can be found on **Max Roach Plus Four** (Emarcy). All nine show that the band recovered from Clifford Brown's tragic loss: at times Dorham's honeyed tones are hauntingly reminiscent of the man he replaced.[52]

In April Rollins returned to Blue Note's studios for **Volume Two,** which harked back to his beginnings in reuniting him with his first significant, J.J. Johnson. Having eschewed the piano altogether for **Way Out West,** Rollins now decided to use two pianists on *Mysterioso* – composer Monk and Horace Silver. The idea was characteristically bold and could have been messy: in the event it comes off triumphantly. The playing is adventurous and intense; at the same time everything is very well-organised. Monk starts and finishes – his work behind Rollins is especially fine – while Silver takes over on Johnson's entry half-way through. The transitions are as smooth as could be, and the fierce brilliance of the music is rooted in Rollins's unerring sense of structure. Monk also shines on *Reflections* (where Johnson and Silver are absent) while the Monk-less quintet perform four numbers of satisfying range and depth.

By the time his next studio date came along, Rollins had branched out on his own, although on occasion he appeared in Miles Davis's group, as John Coltrane had decided to take a year out in order to kick his drug addiction. All his customary wares are on display on **The Sound Of Sonny** (Riverside) – a pianoless *The Last Time I Saw Paris*; two odd-ball songs, *Toot Toot Tootsie, Goodbye* and *Mangos* (a recent hit for Rosemary Clooney); a rewarding partnership with yet another fine pianist – this time Sonny Clark. To all that can be added a new feature: the unaccompanied tenor solo. Coleman Hawkins had showed the way with his famous 1949 *Picasso*;[53] Rollins 'replies' with *It Could Happen To You*, a performance of signal authority that may resemble Hawkins in spirit but is entirely personal in style.

The fall of 1957 saw five sessions that together document the full range of Rollins's mature art. **Newk's Time**, a quartet date cut in September for Blue Note is in the main classic hard bop, though Rollins the radical resurfaces on *Surrey With The Fringe On Top*, which is a superb duet for tenor and drums (Philly Joe Jones). Elsewhere Rollins is fluent and relaxed, revelling in the support of Wynton Kelly and bassist Doug Watkins; once again, as Jack Cooke astutely observes, he "manages to be at once spontaneous yet highly organised."[54] Though not quite as magnificent as **Saxophone Colossus**, the album approximates it in both achievement and ethos: insofar as one can speak of the 'standard Rollins' during this period, **Newk's Time** is the definitive specimen. In November and December two remarkably disparate projects dramatised other aspects of his work and nature.

All the music on **A Night At The Village Vanguard** (Blue Note, two CD volumes) was taped on November 3, but it is also a distillation of an engagement that found Rollins at his most mercurial. In the words of the original release's annotator Leonard Feather:

> Sonny spent his weeks at the Vanguard experimenting, toying briefly with the idea of using a quintet. For the first week he had trumpet, piano, bass, drums and himself. The second week he dropped the trumpet and brought in a new rhythm section.
>
> Still not feeling that he was quite the right presentation, he wound up with an economy-sized combo that turned out to be the most satisfactory to him – the tenor sax-bass-drum trio heard on these sides.[55]

Even then Rollins remained somewhat indeterminate or restless: the majority of the sixteen tracks feature Wilbur Ware and Elvin Jones, but on a few they are replaced by Donald Bailey and Pete LaRoca. Given that background and those names, the music is everything one would expect – audacious and often startling, torridly intense, profoundly exploratory, but rarely serene. Compared to **Newk's Time** it is very hard work for the listener – full of rewards, naturally, but remorseless and even bleak at times. Curiously, Rollins seems more comfortable with LaRoca than with Jones: the takes of *Night in Tunisia* and *Softly As In A Morning Sunrise* with the former produce Rollins's most assured (if not necessarily his most invigorating) playing of the collection. Ronald Atkins's reflections are very persuasive:

> Despite the remarkable success of parts of the (session), I wonder if Rollins enjoyed working with Jones; when they met again on a 1966 record **East Broadway Rundown** the outcome was none too auspicious ... (On) *Sonnymoon For Two* Jones threshes about to great effect, and he and Rollins indulge in some titanic 4-bar exchanges towards the end. This track is the closest Rollins and Jones come to each other; for the rest, they go their own brilliant ways. Perhaps the music succeeds because of the tension created by powerful opposing forces who are resilient enough to survive each other's company.[56]

Sonnymoon For Two is indeed a towering performance, and the impact of *Old Devil Moon* is also formidable. But while the "tension" that Atkins identifies was productive in the way he indicates, the word also – and obviously – connotes a lack of relaxation and ease. We're a long way here from the genially experimental **Way Out West** or the magisterial assurance of the Silver-Monk *Mysterioso*: the mood is febrile rather than celebratory. For all its many riches, **A Night At The Village Vanguard** is characterised by anxiety.

The contrast with Rollins's next recordings is both stark and instructive. Five weeks after the Village Vanguard sessions, he was in Verve's studios alongside Dizzy Gillespie and backed by the Bryants (Ray and Tommy) on piano and bass and drummer Charlie Persip; eight days later Sonny Stitt joined them for a sextet date. These sessions showcase Rollins's 'mainstream' persona; maybe that is why they have received scant attention from those who chiefly value his more experimental side. If so, that is their loss, as Collier has trenchantly observed:

> I think it unfortunate that Rollins felt it necessary to experiment as much as he did. When he permitted himself to play straightforward hard bop, he could be a magnificent improviser...(The) set with Dizzy Gillespie and Sonny Stitt ... contains a fourteen-minute cut called *The Eternal Triangle*, and it represents a peak of hard-driving ferocity in this style ... He demonstrates that he is capable of that extraordinary inventiveness, that tumbling outpouring of phrases that characterises the work of both his mentors Hawkins and Parker. Here there is none of the broken, jagged phrasing that he used on *Blue Seven* and other pieces.[57]

My only demur would be to argue that Rollins's stop-choruses on *I Know That You Know* from the same session transcend even the brilliance of *The Eternal Triangle*. On the former Rollins launches into his solo with a torrential energy that suggests he could hardly wait for the unison theme statement to end. His improvisation lasts exactly one and one-third minutes: it remains arguably the most exciting eighty seconds of tenor on record, and for all the quality of Stitt and Gillespie's subsequent solos, they have in effect been eclipsed before they start.

Both Gillespie dates abound in spendour. Rollins is at his most aggressive on the quintet's *Wheatleigh Hall*, yet repeated listening reveals how beautifully designed his solo is, its smooth logic the perfect counterweight to the piece's attacking lines and fierce tempo. In contrast he recalls Gene 'Jug' Ammons,[58] in his lazily voluptuous phrasing on the slow blues *Sumphin'* (quintet) and is similarly commanding on the analogous *After Hours* (sextet), unimprovably set up by Ray Bryant's famous prelude. The latter was once an r-&-b hit, and thus restores Rollins to his roots in 'good time music'. And it is indeed resplendently evident that Rollins *enjoyed* these Gillespie-Stitt collaborations. Authority pours out of him, but so does *joie de vivre* – a quality vital to his imperious form on *I Know That You Know*. It's worth repeating that the Pleasure Principle lies at the heart of all his finest work.

If I pass quickly over **The Freedom Suite**, Rollins's next recording (for Riverside), that is only because it is analyzed in detail in Part Four, both musically and contextually. It was his most ambitious project yet, and an appropriate way in which to commemorate his magnificent partnership with Max Roach – one that was spiritual as well as musical. It was Roach who memorably defined jazz as "America's true classical music"[59], a nobly ideological view with which Rollins undoubtedly concurred; both men also possess a dignified but profound political idealism. As telegraphed, all that will be explored in full later; for now, it will suffice to suggest that Freedom Suite was a mighty and, it seemed, auspicious start to Rollins's '58.

In fact his recording activity turned out to be a lot less intensive than in the previous two years. There was no diminution in quality; but a fascinating anecdote throws some light on why the reduction in quantity came about – and also, perhaps, on why Rollins began his long sabbatical the next year.

Originally Rollins was contracted to make at least four albums for Verve – the two Gillespie sessions and two dates to be supervised by Leonard Feather. The first of these was **Trio/Brass** (q.v.) comprising four big band sides and four trio ones featuring Henry Grimes on bass and drummer Charles Wright. The second was scheduled to be a full trio date, also with Grimes and Wright, but it never materialsed. In *The Jazz Years*, Feather relates the strange story of how Rollins ensconced himself in Los Angeles, called Feather full of enthusiasm about setting up the recording, only to cancel on the day arranged for the session. He did not even see Feather personally, instructing his wife to tell him, "I'm sorry, Sonny just doesn't feel like recording." Feather concludes: "To this day, I have no idea why this happened." [60] Since the incident took place in the fall of 1958, it is tempting to see such quirky behaviour as foreshadowing Rollins's imminent lay-off: maybe he was approaching saturation point.

The work that Rollins did fulfil for Verve makes that 'missed opportunity' seem all the more regrettable. **Trio/Brass**, excellent anyway, is (as noted earlier) of special significance in being the only big-band date Rollins has ever recorded. The charts are the work of Ernie Wilkins – a wise and prescient choice on Feather's part, for Wilkins would soon provide distinguished scores for both Ray Brown and Oscar Peterson.[61] A writer of great craft and considerable subtlety, Wilkins has always made deft use of the tuba in his arrangements, and here Don Butterfield's work is a telling addition to the other top NYC brass men.

The material is a typical Rollins mixture – a custom-made Wilkins chart, *Far Out East*; a vigorous standard, Gershwin's *Who Cares?;* a Rollins original, *Grand Street*; and the by-now-expected maverick choice, in this case *Love Is A Simple Thing*. Rollins and the orchestra take this last joyously apart, with the tenorist at his most insouciantly authoritative. There are also good solos from Clark Terry and Belgian guitarist René Thomas,[62] and in all it seems absurd that this remains Rollins's only outing with a large aggregate. He plays as to the manner born. and throughout there is an air of uncomplicated delight: the interplay between Wilkins's athletic scoring and Rollins's rasping, good-humoured invention is particularly gratifying.

In the summer of 1958 Rollins renewed musical acquaintance with John Lewis, recording inter alia the aforementioned *Doxy* and a notably tender *You Are Too Beautiful.* (Both can be found on the Verve CD compilation **Sonny Rollins and Friends.**) At the same time he sat in with the full MJQ on their **At the Music Inn** concerts. It would be idle to pretend that these tracks are first-division Rollins, but their humour and slightly eccentric charm have endured.

Rollins made one final studio date before bowing out. As a farewell, **Sonny Rollins And The Contemporary Leaders** is at once majestic – he is at his most serenely extrovert, relishing the company of Hampton Hawes, Barney Kessel, Leroy Vinnegar and Shelly Manne – and mystifying: why should someone playing like this be contemplating retirement? The record preserves one of his most bizarre programmes – *I've Told Every Little Star, Rock-A-Bye Your Baby With A Dixie Melody* and *In The Chapel In The Moonlight* rub shoulders with *The Song Is You, Alone Together* and *How High The Moon* – but the lithely joyous readings not only ensure that everything comes off: it all has the unified density one associates with a suite.

For a while Rollins continued to play concerts: some examples are available on CD, of which **In Sweden** (1959; DIW Records) with Grimes and Pete LaRoca is probably the best. He also took part in the Playboy Jazz Festival in the summer of 1959. By the fall, however, he had withdrawn completely: it would be two years before he re-emerged.

***

Why did he do it? The short answer seems to be that nobody knows, not even Rollins himself. A lot had happened to him, quickly and very intensively, and only the unimaginative would discount the simple possibility that he needed a rest. Furthermore, he had already established himself as the kind of artist who periodically needs to retrench; after over three years of sustained and concentrated brilliance, he was due for a fallow time. As has been noted along the way, too, Rollins had had his fair share of 'personal problems', of tragedy and frustration, and those things continued to trouble him, muddying his sense of himself as a musician. A diffident man, he was more uncertain of his musical judgment than many less gifted artists. Or he may have felt the need to re-consider his whole life.

There is a further explanation. Rollins's diffidence extended to the frequent concern that someone else might 'take over'. His attitude was never jealous in any ordinary sense; still less was it mean or crabby. But Rollins has always been acutely sensitive to what others, particularly tenorists, are doing, and the rapid advent of John Coltrane clearly got to him, as did the attendant, equally rapid burgeonings of Ornette Coleman and 'Free Jazz'. It is feasible that a determination not to be left behind clinched Rollins's decision to take two years off when apparently at the height of his powers. If so, I believe it was a mistaken course; to justify that assertion I return to 1956 and *Tenor Madness*.

Earlier I called the title "silly" and I stick unrepentantly to that; I've also argued that if *Tenor Madness* is appraised as a 'cutting contest', then Rollins was the clear winner. However, there is evidence to suggest that Rollins himself did not see it in this way. He was by now feeling Coltrane's pressure. He even complained about it – not about Coltrane, but about critics who favoured confrontational styles of comparison: this did considerable damage to musicians, making them feel nervous or even hunted.[63] He was also well aware that Coltrane now occupied the very slot he had turned down because (surely mistakenly) he had not considered himself 'ready' – the tenor chair in Miles Davis's seminal Quintet.[64]

I dislike easy paperback psychology and loathe the slick adoption of superficially convenient 'tags'. Nonetheless, it strikes me that *Tenor Madness* is in one respect uncomfortably apposite after all. Rollins looked on that meeting in particular and Coltrane's presence in general as a threat: that, if not "mad", was unnecessarily neurotic. He was so bothered about what Coltrane was intimating that he forgot the things that he, Sonny Rollins, could do and was doing so superlatively. The rest of **Tenor Madness,** *sans* Coltrane, proves that incontrovertibly. The quartet tracks with Garland-Chambers-Jones are, to repeat, *lovely*: Coltrane was to need a few years before that adjective could regularly and confidently be applied to his work. And it is cruelly ironic that by the time that happened he had indeed overtaken Rollins, not just as 'top tenor' but as a master musician in complete command of his vision and technique and how to marry the two.

After Coltrane's death, Rollins spoke further about *Tenor Madness* in particular and the saxophonist in general with characteristic warmth and generosity. He credited Coltrane with his own adoption of the soprano in the 1970s, saying that Coltrane not only governed the instrument but inspired a host of other players to revere it as a serious member of the saxophone family.[65] But at the time he was aware only of intense pressure, and notwithstanding that string of wonderful 56-58 recordings, he was beginning to feel not only threatened but almost fraudulent. He told that fine critic, the late Charles Fox:

> I was being expected to really deliver great music all the time. My reputation was bigger than what I though I could support with what I was doing and I was getting awfully depressed about it. I just said, "Well, this is it. I just want to work on the things I want to do and get them more under control and then I'll come back." So that's what I did.[66]

That is touching and sad. Rollins may well have found his huge reputation intimidating, but there is precious little evidence that he could not support it with his recorded work: I am far from being alone in regarding that 56-58 period as the apex of his achievement. Furthermore, jazz needed his swinging, complex but joyously fundamental strengths more than it had ever needed such things before. Not only did it lose them at a crucial time: in the intervening years, Rollins himself seemed to question those strengths, deeming it necessary to go in the direction that newer stars and fads were signposting. It took him a long time to recover.

Notes

1 Ira Gitler, *Swing To Bop* (Oxford University Press, 1987), 310.

2 Gore Vidal, "Norman Mailer's Self Advertisements", *On Our Own Now* (London: Panther, 1976), 76.

3 Philip Larkin writing in 1962, reprinted in *All What Jazz* (London: Faber, 1985), 77. No matter that Larkin was a white Englishman writing nearly thirty years after the event: his words precisely dramatise feelings abroad in black communities of the time.

4 Collected on the CD **Piano Starts Here**, Columbia Sony COL 476546.

5 Dave Gelly, *Lester Young* (Tunbridge Wells: Spellmount, 1984), 24.

6 Collected on **Bird's Eyes Volume 1**, Philology 214 W 5.

7 Philip Larkin, ostensibly inimical to Parker in particular and Modernism in general – *vide* the famous introduction to *All What Jazz* – in fact often wrote about him with admiration and penetrating insight. One such moment finds him branding "absurd" the notion that Parker's music was a determined reaction to what had gone before: "As well call leaping salmon a reaction." (*All What Jazz*, 41-2)

8 Quoted in Fox's introduction to his BBC Radio 3 interview with Dizzy Gillespie in July 1988, recorded during Gillespie's visit to England to perform a concert at the Royal Festival Hall with his United Nations Orchestra.

9 See James T. Patterson, *Grand Expectations: The United States, 1945-74* (OUP, 1996).

10 "From Stettin in the Baltic to Trieste in the Adriatic an iron curtain has descended across the Continent (of Europe)." Those famous words of Winston Churchill were part of a speech delivered at Westminster College, Fulton, Missouri on March 5, 1946. They foreshadow – perhaps helped to fuel – the change in America's mood that I speak of. Intriguingly, the phrase "iron curtain" had been used at least three times before – by Ethel Snowden in *Through Bolshevik Russia* (1920), by Churchill himself in a cable of June 4, 1945 to President Truman, and by one Dr. Goebbels in his *Das Reich* (1945).

11 Gitler, *Swing To Bop*, 318.

12 Kitty Grime & Val Wilmer, *Jazz At Ronnie Scott's* (London: Hale, 1979), 72.

13 Joe Goldberg, "Sonny Rollins", *Jazz Masters Of The Fifties* (New York: MacMillan, 1965). Da Capo reprint, 90.

14 *Ibid*, 90; see also the September 1998 CD **Ultimate Coleman Hawkins** (Verve 557 538-2). Rollins chose the sixteen tracks and he also contributes a fascinating and substantial sleeve note. In addition to confirming the story at issue, his comments throughout shed new light on Hawkins's life and art, and it is no exaggeration to say that the essay alone makes the CD a compulsory purchase for admirers of both tenorists.

15 Goldberg, 90.

16 *All What Jazz*, 54.

17 Capitol OU 2006.

18 Capitol (E) CAPS 1024.

19 'Woodshedding' refers to a period of voluntary temporary retirement during which a musician re-thinks his art or refines it through practice.

20 Nat Hentoff & Nat Shapiro, *Hear me Talkin' To Ya* (London: Penguin, 1962), 359.

21 In August 1948 Alger Hiss, the much-respected head of the Carnegie Enowment for International Peace, was 'named' as a 30s Communist by Whittaker Chambers, an erstwhile writer for *Time* magazine. Pursued by the FBI and a rising young Congressman by the name of Richard Nixon, Hiss was eventually cited for perjury and served three years of a five-year sentence, spending more than forty years thereafter protesting his innocence. For a full (and excellent) account, see Patterson, *op cit*, 193-5.

22 Gitler, *Swing To Bop*, 303.

23 Grime & Wilmer, *Jazz At Ronnie Scott's*, 72.

24 Martin Williams, "Sonny Rollins", *The Jazz Tradition* (OUP, 1983), 185-6.

25 The term "hard bop" first enjoyed wide currency in the late 1950s, but the musical features it adumbrates were in evidence earlier. A succinctly authoritative definition is provided by Brian Priestley in *Jazz: The Essential Companion* (London: Grafton, 1987), 215: "The positive aspects of hard bop involved its exaggeration of early bop's polyrhythmic vitality, especially in the accompaniments of band-leaders Art Blakey, Max Roach and Horace Silver, and the resilience of soloists such as Sonny Rollins ...A typical hard-bop composition sounded closer to r & b (but

with post-bop improvisation) *while some even harked back to the 'jump bands' of the 1930s.*" (My emphasis)

26 Richard Cook & Brian Morton, *The Penguin Guide To Jazz On CD, LP & Cassette* (Harmondsworth, 1994), 1111.

27 Max Harrison, Alun Morgan, Ronald Atkins, Michael James & Jack Cooke, *Modern Jazz: The Essential Records* (London: Aquarius, 1975), 47.

28 *All What Jazz*, 199.

29 Grime & Wilmer, *Jazz At Ronnie Scott's*, 84-5.

30 *Ibid*, 85.

31 Before and since, Rollins has made many fine records with another hornman in attendance, but such musicians have either been guests (e.g. Freddie Hubbard on *East Broadway Rundown*), one-off jam session partners (Dizzy Gillespie, Sonny Stitt, Branford Marsalis) or sidemen who are not in his league (Clifton Anderson of late, Bennie Maupin in the 70s). The only possible exception is trumpeter Don Cherry, with whom Rollins worked in 1962-3, but that collaboration lacked the intensity and sheer frequency of his November 55-June 56 partnership with Brown.

32 In conversation with Bob Blumenthal on the sleeve essay for **Ultimate Clifford Brown** (Verve 539 776-2), a selection of Brown's work chosen by Payton himself.

33 On the sleeve to **Work Time**, Prestige P 7126

34 *Reverie* is credited to guitarist Larry Clinton; the true composer, as the sleeve of **Nucleus** acknowledges, is Claude Debussy, who wrote it as a piece for solo piano.

35 Intriguingly, Rollins came to see it this way himself. See below, pp. 51-52.

36 Bailey's account of the friendship between Sobers and Smith is moving and warmly incisive. It comprises Chapter Six of his biography *Sir Gary* (London: Collins, 1976).

37 Gunther Schuller, "Sonny Rollins and the Challenge of Thematic Improvisation", *The Jazz Review*, i / 1 (1958), 6; Williams, *The Jazz Tradition*, 187-90; Goldberg, *Jazz Masters of the Fifties*, 97.

38 James Lincoln Collier, *The Making Of Jazz* (London: Macmillan, 1981), 451.

39 Goldberg, *Jazz Masters Of The Fifties*, 98-9.

40 The same could be said of Stan Getz at a slightly earlier time. The years 1954-5 were something of a personal nightmare for

him: already a heroin addict, he was incarcerated after an abortive attempt to hold up a drugstore; his marriage broke up and his son David sustained multiple skull fractures in a car accident. In the light of all that, his 'post-trauma' recordings are simply astonishing in their grandeur and control. They include the August 1955 meeting with Lionel Hampton where the usually irrepressible vibist in forced into second place, and **West Coast Jazz** made a month later, which contains Getz's now-legendary solo on *Shine*. For a fuller discussion of this music and how it belies the circumstances in which it was made, see my *Stan Getz* (London: Apollo, 1988).

41 Cook & Morton, *The Penguin Guide To Jazz On CD, LP & Cassette*, 1109.

42 Whitney Balliett, *The Sound of Surprise* (Harmondsworth: Penguin, 1963). See especially the Introduction, 9-12.

43 Recorded March 7 – just seventeen days before Ornette Coleman completed another Contemporary album, **Something Else**. Coleman's ground-breaking experiments would soon exert a profound influence on jazz in general and Sonny Rollins in particular.

44 On the sleeve essay to **Way Out West,** Contemporary S7530.

45 Nor for nothing was one of Rollins's favourite tenorists Don Byas, who likewise married the aggression of Hawkins to Young's tonal and rhythmic innovations.

46 Within a year Manne would be the drummer on Ornette Coleman's Contemporary album *Tomorrow Is The Question*.

47 Michael Jarrett, 'The Tenor's Vehicle: Reading *Way Out West*", in Krin Gabbard (ed), *Representing Jazz* (Durham: Duke University Press, 1995), 270.

48 *Ibid*, 270.

49 See above, p 19.

50 Organist Jimmy Smith, always an astute listener as well as a *sui generis* virtuoso, included *I'm An Old Cow Hand* on **Bashin'**, his first date for Verve in 1962. A trio piece, it works very well, and the debt to Rollins is clear.

51 On the sleeve essay to **Way Out West.**

52 These sessions turned out to be some of the last Rollins made with Roach. The tenorist left the band in May 1957 and they were never again regular confrères – though they were reunited in 1958 for one of Rollins's most important projects, **The**

Freedom Suite. See Part Four.

53 Currently to be found on **The Verve Story**, 4-CD Box Set, 314 521 737-2 and also on Verve 557 538-2 (see note 14 above).

54 *Modern Jazz: The Essential Records*, 79.

55 On the sleeve note to **A Night At The Village Vanguard**, Blue Note CDP 7 46517/8 2.

56 *Modern Jazz: The Essential Records*, 82.

57 Collier, 452.

58 Son of the famous boogie-woogie pianist Albert Ammons and another of Rollins's favourite tenor players.

59 Nat Hentoff, *The Verve Story*; insert to **Dizzy Gillespie At Newport**, Verve 2304 348 (LP).

60 Leonard Feather, *The Jazz Years* (London: Pan, 1988), 205.

61 viz **Ray Brown With The All-Star Big Band Featuring Cannonball Adderley** (January 1962: reissued on Verve 314 533 259-2) and **The Oscar Peterson Trio Bursting Out With The All-Star Big Band** (June 1962; now on Verve 314 529 699-2).

62 Thomas, who died in 1975, is amongst the more important musicians Europe has produced, and it is a matter for regret that his discography is not more extensive. He also shines on Stan Getz's March 1971 session, **Dynasty**, recorded at Ronnie Scott's Club (Verve 839 117-2).

63 See Goldberg, *Jazz Masters Of The Fifties*, 102.

64 I say "surely mistakenly" on two counts: the quality of his recorded work hitherto, and the fact that he was Davis's first choice.

65 Actually, although Rollins is doubtless correct in attributing such inspiration to Coltrane, it was Steve Lacy who first revived the soprano sax, in his mid-50s recordings with Cecil Taylor. See especially **In Transition**, recorded at the Newport Jazz Festival.

66 Quoted in the Introduction to BBC Radio 3's broadcast of Rollins's concert at the Fairfield Hall, Croydon, July 1987.

WHAT'S NEW?: 1961-67

Let the word go forth from this time and place, to friend and foe alike, that the torch has passed to a new generation of Americans.

From the inaugural address of President J.F.Kennedy, 1961

From time to time there occurs an unwitting co-operation between history and arithmetic whereby the end of a decimally-designated period coincides with a perceptible shift in ethos and direction. The United States of the 1950s furnishes an ostensible exemplar. The end of the decade saw the exit of Eisenhower and the advent of a new President who happened to be the most glamorous figure politics in the modern age has produced: John Fitzgerald Kennedy. Historian Hugh Brogan succinctly captures the national mood, even if the sardonic undertone is all his own:

> It was a moment for joy: joy in the glitter of the new administration, in the high spirits of the President, the beauty of his wife, the obvious intelligence, energy and devotion of his ministers; in the strength and splendour of America at her height, queen and dynamo of the nations. Eisenhower went quietly back to his farm at Gettysburg. Nobody foresaw that his bumbling, peaceful reign would ever be looked back on fondly.[1]

It was a time of new hope, of investment in the young and the free and the brave. And if that sentence sounds like an extract from a Democratic Party press release, that is deliberate. Reality never began to match the rhetoric: the heady sense of promise many inferred from Kennedy's inaugural words[2] soon evaporated. As Brogan wryly observes, joy was momentary, and long before Kennedy's assassination in November 1963 America was in many respects a grim and confused land.

It could be said that disillusionment was bound to set in sooner or later. Any government at any time would have found daunting the major problems which the Kennedy administration inherited - the Cold War in general and Berlin in particular; the new communist regime in Cuba; a backlog of overdue reforms; an explosive racial situation; and what was perceived as an escalating crisis in South East Asia. To retain full credibility by solving all those was always going to be a mighty, perhaps impossible task. But three things about Kennedy ensured that he would be additionally and severely hampered.

One was a quality that on the surface seemed a great asset - his oft-cited charisma and the 'Camelot' aura that he and his advisors manufactured so adroitly. This may have been exciting, sexy, almost magical; it was not, however, all that commensurate with such events as the Bay of Pigs fiasco. The second - an almost inevitable consequence of the first - was an increasing tendency to substitute style for substance, which in turn led to a lack of direction or clearly perceived purpose. And third, Kennedy was far from the forward-looking liberal that his publicity machine could fabricate if and when the occasion warranted it; on the contrary, there are grounds to suggest that in military matters especially he was a good deal more inflexible than Eisenhower. Central to his political nature was a resolve, as again his inaugural address put it, to "pay any price, bear any burden, meet any hardship, support any friend, oppose any foe to assure the survival and success of liberty." Stirring words: what they boiled down to was a determination to pursue the Cold War with the utmost rigour. Not for nothing were these the years when America became catastrophically involved in a conflict in Vietnam - a war she was to lose (the first such experience in her history) and whose lasting trauma remains to this day a tragically significant part of many Americans' lives.

Indeed, the war in Vietnam horribly typifies the decade's pattern of headlong reductiveness. Auguries of crusading fulfilment vanished, replaced by massive confusion abroad and urban upheaval at home - including and especially *racial* mayhem. There were race riots (Detroit in 1967 was a chilling exemplar) which the Kerner Commission chose to call "Civil Disorders". Saddest of all was what the middle-60s did to Lyndon B. Johnson. One of the great reforming Presidents, within a year of his accession he had both created a momentum and fashioned concrete achievements that his predecessor's charismatic bluster never even implied. A vigorous supporter of the civil rights movement and friend of Martin Luther King, his energies were increasingly diverted into the Vietnam war; by the time of his morose abdication in March 1968, that conflict had come to obsess him and he had turned against King for daring to question administration policy - so much so that he and the egregious Head of the FBI, J.Edgar Hoover, became close allies in an attempt to discredit and indeed ruin King's crusading career.

They need not have bothered. In 1968 King was assassinated; so was Robert Kennedy. That year saw also the appalling shambles that was the Democratic Convention in Chicago, and what more than a few would come to see as a disaster as large as the Vietnam war itself - the election of Richard Nixon as President. It seemed that America was by now so beset by panic and a sense of disintegration that its only recourse was to choose a proven conservative (later also to be proved a crook) in the desperate faith that he could lead them into calmer, clearer times. Its hopes soured and its energies wildly distorted, the USA was in a state of deep crisis.

American jazz during the decade followed an uncomfortably parallel course. By 1960 the music was arguably in its prime; that is certainly the view of Dave Gelly:

> Looking back on the 1956-60 period ... it seems an impossibly rich and burgeoning time for jazz. From George Lewis to Miles Davis, almost every style could be experienced live, played by its authentic masters. The very oldest jazz musicians had barely reached the age of seventy, and most were in the prime

of life. The one element common to all [was] a kind of expansiveness, an ease and lightness of spirit that comes from knowing one's trade and exercising it in congenial company, without fuss or formality. Across the gulf of the years, and in a very different time, such unpretentious eloquence can be unbearably touching.[3]

Missing here is a roll-call of those who died during the latter 50s - amongst them Parker, Tatum, Young and Billie Holiday - the 1957 demise of Norman Granz's JATP or the separate sojourns away from American jazz undertaken by Stan Getz (playing in Scandinavia) and Sonny Rollins (not playing in New York). But Gelly's account is affecting and cogent, and its celebratory tone is justified. Jazz had long since ceased to be the pop music of the nation, but its health as a minority art form was good. It had survived the advent of rock 'n' roll, the creation of a new market for the young and indeed the evolution of the "teenager" (a word not coined until 1956). New and exciting things seemed to be just around the corner.

And indeed they were. Thanks in part to the comprehensive reissue programmes recently launched by Columbia-Sony, RCA-Bluebird, Impulse! and above all Verve, it is now clear that the early 60s was an extraordinarily rich time for jazz. It may have lacked the kind of serenity implicit in Gelly's above appraisal, and his "unpretentious" is inappropriate to what some 60s musicians were up to, but it had enormous energy and imagination (properly directed in the main), and it was commercially attractive too.[4] And all styles of jazz flourished. Verve, for example, sponsored notably radical projects by Gil Evans, Gary McFarland, Lalo Schifrin, Oliver Nelson, Dizzy Gillespie and Stan Getz & Eddie Sauter; technical experiments such as Bill Evans's multi-dubbed **Conversations With Myself**; what amounted to a complete refurbishment of Jimmy Smith's art and career; a string of superb studio albums by the piano trios led by Oscar Peterson, Bill Evans, and Wynton Kelly; and the company also committed itself to ensuring that mainstream jazz - e.g. Ben Webster, Johnny Hodges and the Count Basie Orchestra - had a proper hearing. The same catholic range also characterised the catalogues of CBS and RCA.

As the decade progressed, however, the situation changed. For reasons to be explored shortly, the major companies' commitment to jazz underwent a sharp reduction; furthermore, a number of artists formed independent associations and began to insist on full creative control in their recording sessions - one of several important ways in which jazz became politicised during this time. Musicians had invariably regarded the jazz business with suspicion anyway, despite the benevolent vision of men like Norman Granz, John Hammond and Blue Note's Alfred Lion. Now some were determined to assert their authority over what the released product might be and their financial and aesthetic stake in it. Thus emerged such organisations as AACM (Association for the Advancement of Creative Musicians), the Jazz Composers' Orchestral Association in NYC, and the Art Ensemble of Chicago. Smaller, independent labels started to flourish: Blue Note, Riverside and Prestige had of course been around for a long time, but during the 60s they were augmented by Milestone, MPS and ECM in Europe, and a company founded in 1960, Impulse!.

The producer of Impulse!'s first sessions was Creed Taylor, who then went to Verve in 1961 when Granz sold the label to MGM. The connection is interesting, because for a while Impulse! (subsequently under the direction of Bob Thiele) embraced a broad policy very similar to Verve's. The company taped a host of albums by Ellington, Gil Evans, Nelson, Webster, Benny Carter, Terry Gibbs, Gary McFarland, Paul Gonsalves and Coleman Hawkins; it also signed John Coltrane, McCoy Tyner and, a little later, Sonny Rollins. But for all the quality of those enterprises - and many are works of high distinction - Impulse! became ineluctibly associated with the most significant jazz force of the decade, which it was decisive in launching under the slogan "The New Wave of Jazz is on Impulse!". This was the explosively contentious 'New Thing", headed by Coltrane, Cecil Taylor and Archie Shepp.

The New Thing was a determinedly radical movement. Musically, it pursued and extended the experiments Ornette Coleman had instigated in the late 1950s. Tonality was questioned, as were all conventional types of structure; great emphasis was placed on heterophony, or on what these days might be described as 'differently aural' experience. In my view the New Thing also - unlike Coleman - forsook jazz's most fundamental property: swing. Its champions argued that it restored to jazz a proper degree of collective improvisation for the first time since the 1920s and in addition "reasserted the primacy of melody."[4] Detractors dismissed these claims, finding the new sounds alien and horrible and condemning its alleged freedom as mere chaos. Thirty-plus years on, the two camps still exist. Moreover, The New Thing embodied an idiosyncratic traditionalism which irritated quite a number of committed jazz enthusiasts otherwise respectful of its aims. It was determined to dig *back* as well, to re-mine the workings of the past, and this alienated (for political as well as musical reasons) those who wanted to go forward and up.

Even a pronounced agnostic would be silly to maintain that the New Thing was all bad or that its consequences were entirely regrettable. It enlarged the vocabulary of jazz, and its avowed determination to go outside conventional ideas of form and harmony led to some exciting innovation. In addition, its iconoclasm could be refreshing - Archie Shepp's sardonic disembowelment of *The Shadow Of Your Smile* remains a classic in its fashion - and its rethinking of ensemble concepts and instrumentation was undoubtedly creative, leading eventually to such marvellous outfits as the World Saxophone Quartet and the David Murray Big Band. But it was not long before the New Thing was faced by the inner contradictions of the very freedom it celebrated. As Matthew Arnold observed, "Freedom is a very good horse to ride, but to ride *somewhere*"; having dismantled or by-passed all 'normal' paths, New Thing musicians discovered there was nowhere else to go. No matter what individual characteristics may have been used by other musicians and thus absorbed into the language of jazz as a whole, the New Thing was and is a *cul de sac*.[5]

The movement's agenda was as much political as musical. More than a few of its practitioners - notably Shepp and dramatist/critic LeRoi Jones - closely aligned themselves with Stokely Carmichael and Black Power, 'racialising' jazz in a fashion both aggressive and new. By and large, despite the profusion of (true) stories about the prejudice and indeed hatred that black musicians have had to endure, the community of jazz musicians themselves has almost always been an egalitarian one. Bebop provides a focal example. Its origins may partly have lain in a racial resentment and a determination on the part of rising black musicians to create a music that no untalented white could steal; nevertheless, if you were white and could play, you were accepted. Zoot Sims remembered those days fondly -

> I think I was fifteen years old ... and if they saw you with a [saxophone] nobody bothered you – a kind of respect. Everything was fine.[7]

– and speaking in 1976 Oscar Peterson echoed and in effect codified the original Beboppers' attitudes:

> I've always said that talent of any kind comes in a variety of colours - black, white, brown, yellow; tall, short; fat, thin; monster-like or gentle.[8]

Peterson practised what he preached. When criticised in 1953 for hiring a white guitarist (Herb Ellis) instead of one of 'the brothers', he replied with an impassioned lecture on the dangers of Crow Jim (i.e. *reverse* racial prejudice). That kind of commitment to transcending racism of *all* kinds also informed Miles Davis's hiring of Bill Evans and, conversely, Stan Getz giving Horace Silver his first job or providing many crucial opportunities for European jazzmen. One is reminded again of Sonny Rollins's eloquent assertion, "jazz means no barriers"[9].

Shepp and his ilk dissociated themselves from such an ethos. Jazz was black music – "Whatever it is, I call it *mine*", Shepp once said – and whites were a contemptible irrelevance. The manifesto was intellectually puny and musically spurious,[10] and its currency as a tenable ideology lasted a few years at most. In its short time, however, it caused a good deal of dissension within the jazz community which was distressing to witness, and in a more oblique way it did even greater damage.

For the great – and hideous – irony about the New Thing was that it alienated the young black audience. Shepp, Jones and others may have trumpeted the arrival of a fully-conscious black music; the fact is that it appealed largely to white Europeans. It is no accident that the New Thing coincided more or less exactly with a huge increase in the popularity of soul music and the transformation of Tamla-Motown from specialist independent into gigantically successful corporation. Nearly all the brothers didn't want to know about jazz any more; it would be a long time before they returned in any significant numbers.

And that withdrawal had a disastrous commercial effect on *all* kinds of jazz, not just the avant-garde. By 1968 – America's '*annus horribilis*'[11] – the jazz business was in a parlous state. The jazz clubs, those irreplaceable schools for musicians young and old, had been growing fewer in number across the nation; now the process accelerated. In a caustic reference to the New Thing, tenorist Eddie 'Lockjaw' Davis identified one of the reasons behind this rapid recession – "Who is going to pay a second time to hear a guy wearing a sheet go rootle-tootle up and down the scale?".[12] By 1968, too, *Down Beat* felt increasingly obliged to include features on rock and soul musicians; a few years later this (probably inevitable) dilution of its original purpose was confirmed by the change of its sub-title to "The Contemporary Music Magazine".

Worst of all in some ways, the jazz record business both shrank and slumped. I had started buying jazz records in 1964 at the age of seventeen. It wasn't a bad year to begin: amongst the new issues over the next twelve months were now-acknowledged masterpieces such as Peterson's **Night Train**, Bill Evans's aforementioned **Conversations With Myself, Woody Herman 1964, L'il Ol' Groovemaker ... Basie, Miles Davis In Europe, Getz/Gilberto**, Jimmy Smith's **The Cat.** Those are personal favourites: the real point is that several major companies were each releasing up to a dozen jazz records per month; reissues were plentiful too. EMI was the UK's chief distributor: with Columbia, Stateside, Impulse!, Capitol, various budget-priced reissue labels and above all Verve under its umbrella, it provided a feast of good, even great jazz that bit deep into the pocket. Add to all that a similar flow from RCA, Philips, CBS and Mercury, plus the specialist labels, and you have a stall resembling a cornucopia for a young learning jazz enthusiast.

By 1968 this was dramatically no longer the case. EMI had changed hands and its jazz policy had become virtually defunct; issues from Verve, now marketed direct by MGM, grew both fewer and more irregular. Plenty of records continued to appear, but the policies governing releases grew ever-more incoherent, and many artists were poorly served or not recorded at all. Even Oscar Peterson – whose popularity was supposed to extend way beyond the jazz coterie and thus make him an attractive signing – had several years without a recording contract with any public corporation. And the growth of independent labels, healthy in itself, could not disguise the larger truth: rock/pop had taken over more or less completely, and jazz had been swamped.

I have already suggested that, no matter what his private reasons, Rollins's 1959 withdrawal was unfortunate for jazz as a whole: it could ill afford to lose his prime strengths at such a time. I now go on to argue that the broader musical and political developments I have just summarised affected him directly on and after his re-emergence – and that much of that effect was not to the good.

II

You won't be surprised when you hear me ... I'm playing just about the way I did before, only I think much better.

Sonny Rollins to Joe Goldberg, 1961[13]

During 1959-61, rumours abounded as to what Rollins was up to. One of the few that was true concerned his celebrated visits to NYC's Williamsburg Bridge in the small hours of the morning. With disarming simplicity, Rollins later explained that he had wanted somewhere to play where he wouldn't disturb his neighbours, who included a pregnant woman who needed her rest! Other gossip was less reliable. Rollins was back on drugs (untrue), was working out strenuously (overstated[14]), recovering from a nervous breakdown (nonsense), and re-thinking and re-fashioning his entire approach to music and style of playing.

How much one credits that last rumour depends considerably on what one makes of the recordings he made for RCA on his re-emergence.[15] Thanks to the 1997 issue of **The Complete RCA Victor Recordings of Sonny Rollins** one can now assess these with a comprehensiveness not possible before. Six albums ensued: **The Bridge** (January & February 1962); **What's New?** (April & May 1962); **Our Man In Jazz** (July 1962); **Sonny Meets Hawk** (July 15 & 18, 1963); **Now's The Time** (May 5, 1964); and **The Standard Sonny Rollins** (June & July 1964). In addition, three sides Rollins cut in February 1963 appeared on the rather curious **3 For Jazz**, rubbing shoulders with separate sets by Gary Burton and Clark Terry; there were also eleven alternative takes, most of which were issued by French RCA in 1981 as the double-LP **The Alternative Sonny Rollins.**[16] The 6-CD collation may not be quite "complete" – the redoubtable Bruyinckx discography lists two **Bridge** tracks and nine from the June & July 1964 sessions that have yet to see the light of day – but it will more than suffice as a data-base by which to judge Rollins's renascent work.

The original albums were of course issued consecutively – which meant that it was a while before critical reaction took fully coherent shape. Even so, it was clear from early on that opinion was decidedly mixed. Some heard an exciting new creativity, detecting an elastic revision of his previous style that had assimilated the essence of 'Free Jazz' while preserving the strengths of hard bop. Others found most of the music disappointing and regressive, evincing a lack of assurance and an unwelcome new harshness. A third school of thought concluded that there was little discernible difference, and that Rollins's sabbatical had turned out to be a supreme non-event.

It is hard to go along with that last view. For a start, as Joe Goldberg observes, whatever the musical reasons for his lay-off may have been, Rollins had

> ... also, of course, perpetrated the greatest possible publicity stunt. To a fan, the only thing more exciting than talent is talent that rejects the public rewards of its fulfilment.[17]

Goldberg is quick to point out that Rollins "does not think in those terms"; as he also remarks, however, that didn't matter much. Enormous public interest had been created in his eventual return: the jazz world was agog for what epiphanies it might witness. And from the outset his re-appearance was a high-profile affair. Although he warned that while away he had been chiefly concerned with "an exploration of the horn", many awaited the revelation of a new style.

Critic Barry McRae was one who discerned a radical freshness, welcoming the RCAs as the work of a newly galvanised musician who had absorbed the innovations of Ornette Coleman while remaining true to his roots. In particular he hailed the meeting with Coleman Hawkins, and was full of praise too for the semi-avant-garde date with trumpeter Don Cherry. Martin Williams was less convinced, but still positive and welcoming. Brian Priestley – a lifelong champion of Rollins's genius and author of some of the best accounts of his work – felt that Rollins had now ceased to be reliable and in some respects had gone awry. And James Lincoln Collier was oracular in his finality of judgment:

> He had come back too late. People were disappointed: they had expected something new, and Rollins was only doing what he had always done, if perhaps with more confidence.[18]

Vestigial admiration clashes with real sadness: that is Collier's last sentence on Rollins in *The Making Of Jazz*.

My own view is separate from all those, although it could be seen as a selective amalgam of them. Priestley strikes me as closest to the mark, although I'd want to add two observations. First, Rollins had always been somewhat mercurial, ideologically committed to experiment, and after two years away it was natural that he should want to try out a whole lot of new ideas; furthermore, that was absolutely in keeping with the times, given the mid-50s innovations effected by Cecil Taylor, the imminence of the New Thing and the exploratory work of Coleman, Coltrane and Eric Dolphy. And if as a 'mini-*oeuvre*' the RCAs exhibit considerable restlessness, that was also true of a fair amount of Rollins's pre-furlough work.

My second point is the one that really bothers me and always has: the strangely *muted* quality of Rollins's refashioned musical personality. The RCAs contain many searingly memorable performances, but his irresistible virility and kinetic bounce are much less in evidence; above all, gone is the voluptuous swagger that so distinguished his previous work. Regrettable anyway, that loss also prompts the thought that Collier's suggestion that the emergent Rollins played "with more confidence" is simply not true.

It is time to consider the albums in detail. During my earlier discussion of Rollins's 1957 recordings I remarked that he evidently wished to draw regular attention to both 'sides' of his musical nature, even to the extent of highlighting them alternately. A very similar pattern characterises the first two RCAs, **The Bridge** and **What's New?** The former, a satisfying *pot pourri* – three standards, a couple of invigorating originals and an uncommonly moving reading of *God Bless The Child* – showcases the more conservative Rollins. What novelty there is hinges on style rather than content. The programme is a typical Rollins mixture, no more adventurous than his 50s selections; indeed, *The Bridge* itself is based on the chords of *I Got Rhythm* – the epitome of bebop practice. Nothing wrong with that, naturally, but it is hardly the stuff of revolutionaries. In sharp contrast, the titular question mark in **What's New?** might well have been deleted as needlessly modest or apologetic.[19] This is Rollins the innovator fashioning a brave essay in rhythmic experiment that also encompasses a startling range of material and ensemble forms.

Its residual conservativism notwithstanding, **The Bridge** enshrines one notable innovation. Rollins had of course worked in pianoless groups before, but this was the first time he replaced the instrument with a guitar. He chose Jim Hall – on the surface a surprising move, but in the event a perspicacious and inspired one. Hall's undoubted lyricism and loveliness of sound are rooted in a sophisticated harmonic mastery and a profound interest in composition. Like Rollins himself, he has the ability to anticipate forthcoming harmonies in his phrasing, and both his use of space and the condensed way in which he can fill it proved a perfect foil. Hall's recollections of their collaboration are as incisive as his playing:

> [Rollins] had all the good elements of music in his playing – compositional elements like taking a small idea and really developing it ...it was sort of like what Picasso did with a face: he'd just turn [a tune] every which way... It was frightening sometimes that I'd have to play after him, except that the music was so good that it was fun to get into it... I think ideally Sonny wanted it to be four-part music and that we

> should react to one another, but his presence was so strong that there was no doubt who the leader was... *Sonny liked the interplay, but also he was very much the leader.*[20]
>
> (My emphasis)

Ably backed by Bob Cranshaw on bass and Ben Riley or Harry Saunders on drums, Rollins and Hall appeared to have pulled off a triumph.

And yet ... For all its many felicities, the album has never moved, thrilled or riveted me in the way that happens every time I play **Saxophone Colossus, Way Out West** or **Sonny Rollins Plus Four,** to cite just three 50s albums. The energy and authority remain, but the sensual brio and muscular grace have gone. In their place is something newly *effortful*, a quality that Graham Colombé has glossed very well:

> What he plays here seems to challenge his own past as well as his contemporaries' and ... comes over as deliberate and studied rather than flowing or natural.[21]

It is as if Rollins's primary intention was to justify his claim to Joe Goldberg that he was now playing "much better"; I do not think that is the case. And his accompanying observations – "You won't be surprised when you hear me ... I'm playing just about the way I did before" – are similarly questionable when one listens either to **The Bridge** or its radical successor.

No more prevarication. For thirty-plus years I have tried in vain to enjoy **What's New?** As I implied just now, it more than justifies its title: its ambition is commendable, some of Rollins's tonal effects are extraordinary and there is much that compels. But the Pleasure Principle is in short supply. Indeed, the music is for the most part decidedly joyless – an apparently perverse summary of a set that includes *Don't Stop The Carnival* and the analogous *Brown Skin Girl*, but I'll stick to it. The lugubrious is especially prevalent during *Jungoso*, where Rollins is backed by just

Cranshaw and Candido on congas and which for a variety of reasons I would nominate as the album's most noteworthy track.

Loren Schoenberg's essay that accompanies **The Complete RCA** set includes several judgments with which I cannot agree (q.v.) but this one is historically acute and spot-on:

> *Jungoso* must have come as something of a shock to Rollins fans, for nothing in his previous work had hinted at this kind of extreme approach. The tonal distortions heard on (*If Ever I Would Leave You*) are multiplied tenfold ...[22]

The only 50s performances that remotely approximate *Jungoso* are to be found on **A Night At The Village Vanguard,** where Rollins also worked with just bass and drums in a fashion analogously remorseless and bleak. But any real sense of similarity evaporates in the face of one overwhelming difference. *Jungoso* is indeed quite unlike anything Sonny Rollins had done before: it doesn't *swing.*

Now that's what I call "a shock". For quite a while after it hit me I was unwilling to believe my own feet, and well aware that to level such a charge at a Rollins record is to invite outrage, derision or both, I subjected the claim to an exhaustive aural-and-ankle test before committing it to paper. *Jungoso* certainly does not lack rhythmic complexity: Cranshaw's walking bass contrasts with the tenorist's audacious phrasing and the intricate patterns he weaves with Candido, and if it's sheer energy you're after you won't be disappointed. But the kind of irresistible momentum axiomatic (one thought) to the tenorist's every performance is absent.

How much that matters depends, I suppose, on how important you judge swing to be in jazz's scheme of things. It is safe to infer that it did not bother overmuch those who would soon thrill to Shepp and late (i.e. post-Tyner-&-Elvin Jones) Coltrane. But for one like myself who considers swing *the* definitive property of jazz, it matters decisively – the more so when remembering the Rollins of *St. Thomas, I Know That You Know* and *Wagon Wheels*. Moreover, the dearth of swing is compounded by a jagged lack of assurance. Listening to *Jungoso* is a nervy experience not unlike listening to the best of latterday Bud Powell: one is on tenterhooks waiting for fluffs that one prays will not materialise. They don't, but relief is a pale substitute for full satisfaction.

Elsewhere there are the aforementioned *Don't Stop The Carnival* and *Brown Skin Girl*. The former, now as ineluctibly associated with Rollins as *St. Thomas* or *Blue Seven*, is a highly tentative reading compared to later performances of the tune that he would give, especially in concert. The rhythms are supple enough and it certainly swings, but Rollins rarely sounds fully at ease or in charge, and he is in effect upstaged by the (very ordinary) vocal group, who were surely a mistaken addition. Similar remarks apply to *Brown Skin Girl*, a superfically engaging Rollins original which rarely grips. The best playing comes (briefly) from Jim Hall, and to find Loren Schoenberg labelling the tune Rollins's "equivalent of *The Girl From Ipanema*"[23] induces an uncomfortable pathos, even if its conflation of the calypso with the samba 'craze' is pertinent: the two remaining cuts are done as bossa novas.

That embracing of a new form apart, *If Ever I Would Leave You* and *The Night Has A Thousand Eyes* are more conventional than the album's other cuts; they are also more successful. The former is by some distance the album's best track, in fact – melodic, swinging and multiply resonant. However, Schoenberg's observation "There's no way anyone would confuse *this* bossa nova with a Stan Getz album!"[24] is not only gratuitously snooty: it is most unwise, for it invites an examination of the tenorists' contrasting bossa nova achievements that rebounds badly on the author and by association Rollins himself.

The two men became interested in the form at almost exactly the same time. Getz's **Jazz Samba** was recorded in February 1962, just two months before **What's New?**; furthermore, the Rollins-Hall collaboration mirrors that of Getz and guitarist Charlie Byrd, whose idea it was to have Getz play on what had originally been envisaged as a trio date. As noted earlier, **Jazz Samba** was an astounding success, which gave rise to a spate of bossa nova albums pairing Getz with Luiz Bonfa (**Jazz Samba Encore**), Joao and Astrid Gilberto, The Gary McFarland Orchestra (**Big Band Bossa Nova**) and Laurindo Almeida. All sold very well, especially **Getz/Gilberto**, and that offended the kind of jazz purist – still with us – who equates commercial success with loss of integrity and/or aesthetic shallowness: Schoenberg is far from alone in his snootiness.

Getz did get bored with this remorseless studio diet – he sardonically rechristened his most celebrated hit "Dis Here Finado" – but he never renounced the form nor felt any need to apologise for the records themselves. Nor should he have done: they abound with outstanding jazz, and if Schoenberg and his ilk can't hear beyond the surface charm, that is their great misfortune. The instant loveliness of Getz's sound enhances the muscular grace of his phrasing, which is just as imaginative and audacious in its way as Rollins's is in his. Above all, Getz's samba records swing with a lithe ferocity that *Don't Stop The Carnival* or even the excellent *If Ever I Would Leave You* are hard pressed to match. And *The Night Has A Thousand Eyes* provides a direct and revelatory comparison.

Rollins's version is delightful: lissom and relaxed, with Hall at his most incisive, it explores the trenchant harmonies with seemingly lazy mastery. Dialogue between tenor and guitar is witty, affectionate and consistently telling, and there's a sunniness all too absent in *Jungoso* and *Bluesongo*, along with the "unabashed lyricism" that Schoenberg rightly identifies.

Getz recorded the song[25] on May 1st 1969 – i.e. seven years after **What's New?**. The opening bars are not auspicious: Johnny Pate's arrangement favours lush strings and suave brass, and although the pulse is formidable from the outset, the Ghost of Muzak To Come hovers ominously. Then, suddenly, the performance segues into a pile-driving 4/4 stomp. Fuelled by the incomparable Hank Jones on piano and magnificent drums & percussion, Getz's solo is volcanic, inducing in me the kind of reaction that guitarist Herb Ellis often experienced when playing with Oscar Peterson:

> I've never played with anybody who had more depth and more emotion in his playing. He can play so hot and so deep and earthy that it just *shakes* you ... Ray [Brown] and I have come off the stand just shook up. I mean, he is *heavy*.[26]

Not everyone will echo my response to Getz's solo or find the Peterson analogy persuasive. But I do think that anyone checking out *The Night Has A Thousand Eyes* on this 'head-to-head' basis will find the contrast both dramatic and paradoxical: Pretty Boy Getz tears great chunks out of the tune while Hard Bop Dude Rollins caresses it with thoughtful tenderness. It would be grotesquely unfair to Rollins to call his reading anaemic, but in this instance it was Getz who'd eaten all the red meat.

Before leaving **What's New?**, a last word about its incarnation on CD, where it happens to be followed by two **Alternative Sonny Rollins** cuts, *52nd Street Theme* and *Four*, recorded early in 1964. The latter is more than decent, but the former is absolutely wonderful – a staggering fifteen minutes of unflagging creativity, on-the-edge artistic courage and exhilarating power. He is accompanied by drummer Roy McCurdy and bassist Ron Carter – who just six days before (February12) provided his regular boss Miles Davis with exactly the kind of relentless brilliance he furnishes here.[27]

52nd Street Theme is of course a Thelonious Monk composition, and here one sees the further benefit of their many collaborations in the 1950s. Few players have penetrated and absorbed Monk's music as comprehensively as Rollins, and that loving understanding serves him well. The trio nearly breaks down after about six minutes, but they retrench and re-launch the performance with superb panache; four minutes later the exchanges between tenor and drums are breathtaking in both invention and coherent snap. Rollins's wit surfaces regularly amidst his furious examination of Monk's tune – there are beautifully judged quotations from *Blue Moon* and *Swanee River* – and in sum the performance has all the majesty of the 'old' Rollins allied to increased urgency and a new harmonic daring. And while I have no wish to pillory **What's New?** – an honourably compelling album no matter what its drawbacks – it is nonetheless extraordinary that something so evidently superior as *52nd Street Theme* had to wait seventeen years for release anywhere and nearly thirty in Rollins's own land.

A browser glancing at Rollins's next RCA session, **Our Man In Jazz**, might infer a modest, even perfunctory affair: three tracks only. In fact, the LP weighed in at nearly fifty minutes – a considerable figure in those days. Our browser might also conclude from the material (two old Rollins favourites, *Oleo* and *Doxy*, and a standard, *Dearly Beloved*, that appeared on **The Sound of Sonny**) that the album resuscitates Rollins's conservative *persona*. Again, not so – and that's putting it mildly. **Our Man In Jazz**, recorded live at New York's Village Gate, remains Rollins's most sustained investigation of 'free' jazz; to this end he hired half the Ornette Coleman Quartet, trumpeter Don Cherry and drummer Billy Higgins, to whom he added the ever-dependable Cranshaw.

The album preserves some stunning music. Higgins is superlative throughout, there is much distinguished work from both horns, and overall it is both more organically-realised and more successful than **What's New?**, while offering even less in the way of serene enjoyment. The twenty-five minute *Oleo* is at times uncomfortably demanding, and the other selections are no less intense for being much shorter. Cherry's work is very impressive: while he will never be my favourite trumpeter, there is no doubting the fertility of his imagination and few musicians have had a quicker brain. Rollins responds with enormous vigour and competitive élan, and although it often seems frenetic the music swings from start to finish.

There is, however, one thing conspicuously absent on this date: any sense of an authentic front-line *partnership*. We are a world away here from the Rollins-Brown sides – not just in style (that's obvious enough) but in what might be termed the working ethic. Cherry and Rollins go very much their own way: they may inspire each other (q.v.) but they do not feed off each other. Indeed, I am reminded of those remarks by Ronald Atkins on Rollins's collaboration with Elvin Jones on the **Village Vanguard** date five years before:

> ... They go their own brilliant ways. Perhaps the music succeeds because of the tension created by powerful opposing forces who are resilient enough to survive each other's company.[28]

Exchanges are minimal, and their approach and values are almost ostentatiously different, prompting Michael Shera to observe

> If Rollins learned anything from his association with Cherry, it was that he would never employ another horn player who stood any chance of giving him real competition.[29]

That is cogent, but any inference that Rollins was put off Cherry by this date would be unjustified. In February 1963 they, and Higgins, were reunited in RCA's studios; Henry Grimes replaced Cranshaw. They recorded three titles, released as Rollins's contribution to **3 In Jazz**, and the same quartet also toured Europe that spring: some of their work is preserved on the two-volumed

Rollins Meets Cherry.[30] The former session is somewhat anticlimactic after the Village Gate set, chiefly because of the pieces' brevity; they are interesting nonetheless, in that all three cuts are standards – *You Are My Lucky Star, I Could Write A Book* and *There Will Never Be Another You* – which are treated radically but with respect. The final tune (which became a staple part of Rollins's mid-60s repertoire) is deconstructed wholesale; unlike the forthcoming *Django* and *East Broadway Rundown,* the approach is entirely vindicated, especially at the close, where Cherry's impish humour is showcased as delightfully as Rollins's customary wit.

The recently unearthed European concert suffers from indifferent sound – prodigious wow and an almost constant under-hum contrast spectacularly with the newly remastered RCAs – but fortunately that does not drown another titanic performance from Higgins or the furious creativity of the hornmen. Rollins is at his most passionately ambitious, and his playing here offers decisive confirmation of how Cherry inspired him to explore his vocabulary and structural instincts to the utmost.

Nevertheless, the long-term facts support Michael Shera's case. In all three dates the emphasis is on cogent monologue rather than symbiotic exchange: it is significant that the one irksome feature of the twenty-minute *52nd Street Theme* on Moon 054-2 occurs when Cherry meddles in Rollins's final cadenza. In making essentially the same point as Shera, Loren Schoenberg concludes:

> Sonny learnt a lot ... from his association with Cherry, and the greatest lesson is possibly what led to the quartet's demise. Like many other great and heroic soloists, Rollins needs to be the principal protagonist ... When confronted with a free spirit such as Cherry, some of his options were foreclosed, and this was to be the last Rollins working date with an artistic peer in the front line.[31]

That last sentence is not entirely accurate: Rollins added the superb Thad Jones on several 1964 selections and Freddie Hubbard shared the spotlight on **East Broadway Rundown**'s title track. But that is to nit-pick. Shera and Schoenberg are both correct in their separate observations that it would be a long time before Rollins employed a regular front-line partner and that even then the men he chose were not in his league. As Jim Hall remarked, for all that Rollins "liked the interplay", by now and from now on "he was very much the leader."

Which makes it all the more surprising that Rollins's very next RCA teamed him with Coleman Hawkins – surprising and in my view regrettable. As always with Rollins the session is replete with interest, but he does not sound at ease alongside his original inspiration. And although Hawkins himself plays very well throughout, Schoenberg's encomium – "one of the best albums [he] made in his last decade"[32] – is not convincing. To compare this album with Hawkins's work on three virtually contemporaneous dates for Impulse! (**Today And Now, Meets Duke Ellington** and Benny Carter's magnificent **Further Definitions**) is not so much salutary as close to embarrassing.

That said, I can see why Schoenberg admires Hawkins's playing here so much. The irony is that it's not the Old Master who is thrown by the pairing but Rollins: he seems, again, determined to show how 'different' he can be rather than freshly to explore his organic relation to Hawk's music. His puckish and brief introduction to the opening *Yesterdays* is well-meant and of course well-executed, but it is rendered immediately inapposite by Hawkins's impassioned solo, and when Rollins re-enters he seems bent on exploring the tenor's tonal properties at the expense of all else. The musicianship is unimpeachable and I have no doubt that Hawkins admired it: as a work of art it is nevertheless inchoate.

The date was an odd one in another way. Why was Paul Bley picked? A fine pianist then making a name for himself as an avant-garde musician, he has good touch and great sensitivity, but for different reasons neither tenorist sounds comfortable with him (though he takes several telling solos, especially on *All The Things You Are*). The glaringly obvious candidate, surely, was Tommy Flanagan, Hawkins's sideman on the aforementioned **Today And Now** and a vital component in the triumphant **Saxophone Colossus.** Perhaps Flanagan wasn't available; alternatively, the fact that Bley was an RCA-contracted artist at the time may have had something to do with it. Whatever the explanation, Bley was, through no fault of his own, an enigmatic and finally unsatisfactory choice. In all, while the album has several moving passages – *Summertime* is especially poignant – as an artistic collaboration it is best described as fitful, confirming rather than confounding Rollins's growing aversion to sharing the spotlight.

Sonny Meets Hawk also raises further questions about RCA's policy towards their prized and very expensive new property – a matter which has always puzzled me. The company triumphed over several competitors to land Rollins's signature (amongst them Riverside, which "had come in third"[33]), and in many respects it deserves enormous credit for the way it represented the tenorist's art. As Schoenberg observes, it was "remarkable" that "a major record company would issue and promote music like this at a time when the Beatles were about to rule the world."

Everything was fine at first. That intriguingly disparate pair, **The Bridge** and **What's New?**, was an intelligent way to launch the 'new' Rollins, making good sense both commercially and aesthetically. RCA should also be congratulated on **Our Man In Jazz**, whose demanding fare was never going to attract a large market: to issue it was as brave and honourable as the music itself. But that very integrity may also have occasioned a revisionist change. Schoenberg observes that any thoughts about "Rollins having a commercial potential must have been dashed by this effort,"[34] and the record may have proved a watershed, persuading RCA's executives that Rollins was 'oddball' rather than 'viable'. That would explain the otherwise baffling Burton-

Terry-Rollins **3 In Jazz** – "the logic of the compilation escapes me" is Schoenberg's suitably tart comment[35] – and the eccentricities that mar **Sonny Meets Hawk.**

Perhaps Rollins himself was confused – about what he wanted to do, the kind of music he wanted to record and with whom, and what precisely was the current state of his art. If so, he recovered well, for his last two RCA albums represent arguably his best work for the company.

Now's The Time was recorded over four sessions in January, February and April 1964 and marries the 'old' and 'new' Rollins in exhilarating fashion. The programme comprises eight modern jazz standards, and although Rollins's improvisatory style is discrete from his 50s work, that fullness of tone makes a happy return, especially on the threnodic *I Remember Clifford*, where, underpinned by Cranshaw and McCurdy, his playing is just gorgeous; this trio also impresses on Gillespie's *Blue 'N' Boogie*. A four-minute *52nd Street Theme* crackles with urgency – McCurdy is superb, and Rollins is much more prepared to engage in dialogue with Thad Jones than he ever was with Cherry. And *Now's The Time* itself a vibrant reading, with Herbie Hancock's piano a welcome bonus – though the alternative take (q.v.) is even better.

Personally, I think the inclusion of *St. Thomas* was a mistake. Admittedly, the two cuts (one not released until French RCA issued **The Alternative Sonny Rollins**) are more than decent: the tenorist's ideas are cogent and fertile, and Ron Carter and Mcurdy support him to near-perfection. It's just that nothing could compete with the *absolute* perfection of Roach, Watkins and Flanagan on the **Saxophone Colossus** original, and that goes for Rollins's work too: he did his 'new' self no favours with this remembrance of times past. On the other hand, *'Round Midnight* is splendid, surviving comparison with all previous Rollins readings, and the brief but riveting *Afternoon In Paris*, with Hancock back at the piano, underlines Rollins's (surprising to some) affinity for John Lewis's music. The session closes with a particular Rollins favourite, Miles Davis's *Four*: backed again by just Cranshaw and McCurdy, the tenorist is at his most commanding, and for all its surface fury the performance is distinguished for its structural logic and sensual glow.

The sessions that led to **Now's The Time** also produced six further cuts that either RCA or Rollins did not want to release at the time. They are without exception fascinating and a crucial addition to the tenorist's discography – which means that French RCA deserves our gratitude for their 1980s release. But it's also not hard to see the rationale behind their original non-appearance. They are avowedly experimental, and it figures that these more extreme readings were judged to be inapposite to the album's ethos – modern classics freshly but recognisably revisited – or were simply considered less successful than the chosen take. That last is certainly true of *St. Thomas*, which is even more markedly inferior to the 1956 original than its stablemate; *Afternoon In Paris*, both more perfunctory and cruder than the first-issued version; and *Four*, which is shorter and less satisfying than its counterpart.

That leaves *Django* and the fifteen-minute *Now's The Time*. Concerning the former, Michael Shera wittily points out that it is "odd to describe this as an alternative as no other RCA version exists," but I cannot share his opinion that it "swings like mad".[36] Hancock, Carter and McCurdy are admittedly excellent, but they cannot camouflage an out-of-sorts Rollins whose chief aim seems to have been a determination to plumb new depths of tonal hideousness. As noted, he usually shines when addressing the music of John Lewis, but not this time. The original's brooding theme and rhapsodic harmonies invite Romantic indulgence: it says much for the MJQ that their many versions almost always avoid that pitfall. But Rollins's extreme deconstruction is in the main just ugly. Despite moments of searing power he treats the theme with an unattractive – and highly uncharacteristic – knowingness which rebounds badly on him. As with Shepp's *The Shadow Of Your Smile* one senses a joke, but this one just isn't funny: Rollins here resembles a debunking adolescent making cheap points. The effect is solely to remind one what an intrinsically distinguished composition *Django* is and to forget about Rollins's reading of it as soon as possible.

Now's The Time is spectacularly a different matter. This is Rollins at his uniquely imperious best, a seemingly inexhaustible fountain of inspiration and driving power: this really *does* "swing like mad". He never repeats himself during his mammoth solo, and responds instantly when Hancock rejoins the fray (the pianist lays out for much of the time). One can see why RCA chose not to issue this cut at the time: its length is forbidding to all but the most dedicated listener, and the music is never less than intensely demanding. But once again it is an aesthetic shame that we had to wait so long to realise what heights Rollins was capable of during his time with the company: *Now's The Time* can stand proudly alongside his 50s work for Blue Note, Riverside and indeed its 'cousin' *Tenor Madness*, even if it is tonally different.

The tenorist's final album for RCA completed another imaginative pairing: the focus in **Now's The Time** on classics of modern jazz was now complemented by a celebration of the popular song (chiefly American) at its best. **The Standard Sonny Rollins** (recorded in June & July 1964) is, however, less uniformally satisfying than its predecessor. That invariably annoying 60s engineering fad – the fade – tarnishes several tracks, lending them an indeterminate air: *Three Little Words* suffers in particular from the practice, and despite some promising ideas this performance is no match for the one Rollins cut a year later for Impulse!. *I'll Be Seeing You* is no more than a fragment, and the not much longer *Autumn Nocturne* and *Night And Day* are in addition buzzy in tone and not fully developed. On the other hand, *My One And Only Love* and, especially, *My Ship* are exquisite: the latter has to rate as one of Rollins's finest collaborations with Jim Hall, and is as beautiful a ballad reading as can be found in his entire discography.

If *My Ship* is the album's masterpiece, *Trav'lin' Light* is its revelation. Two versions were recorded: the originally-issued take lasts just over four minutes, the alternative three times that much. The chief source of interest is the use of two bassists, Teddy Smith (*pizzicato*) and David Izenon *(arco)*. Izenon was part of Ornette Coleman's trio at this time, and both his impact on Rollins's playing and the extraordinary effects his work contributes to the music as a whole are decisive. The short cut is riveting enough, but its extended companion is something else again.[37] Hall and Hancock are at their most thoughtfully lyrical while Izenon's work, superficially weird, becomes ever more haunting with each playing; Rollins's lines, instinctively apposite, weave in and out of this remarkable tapestry, deploying a range of tonal effects united by a governing tenderness.

As has been indicated several times along the way, opinion has always been mixed about Rollins's RCA output, and judging from the reviews of the **Complete** set, it looks like remaining so. At a basic level, it goes without saying that all his work for the company is both important and valuable. As Michael Shera observed at the end of his appraisal –

> ... with a great artist such as Rollins, even the imperfect performances are well worth having.[38]

– and sometimes the imperfections are as fascinating in their way as the triumphs are in theirs. Moreover, the music has lasted well. Yes, there will continue to be disagreements about just how good it is, both in itself and relative to what came before and after, but nobody has ever suggested that it is negligible or demonstrably transient. In a rewarding *Down Beat* article, "Needed Now: Sonny Rollins", Gordon Kopulos, though not entirely enamoured of the tenorist's RCA output, paid this tribute to its power and durability:

> ... in addition to some harmonically incorrect blowing [much of it features] a Sonny Rollins who was already into the avant-

> garde, replete with overtones, squawks and out of tempo free-swinging. By comparison, in fact, much of today's free jazz seems a little atrophied.[39]

Kopulos was writing in 1971, by which time, according to many observers, jazz was in a bad way: hence his article's title. One doesn't have to share that bleak view to look back on Rollins's RCA work with both admiration and affection.

Neverthless, I also think that John Fordham is right in referring to this period as Rollins's "*eminence grise* phase", one noticeably "more vexed and introspective" than his pre-sabbatical work.[40] By and large the RCA work lacks serenity and the absolute assurance of the earlier Blue Notes, Riversides, Verves, Prestiges and so forth. In addition – or perhaps just another way of phrasing the same point – very little of it is *sexy*. And that is no facile or nudging observation: Rollins's greatest work is erotically charged amidst all else, overflowing with vibrancy and earthy affirmation even at its most demanding.

My final observation before moving on to Rollins's post-RCA work hinges on two already-quoted observations by James Lincoln Collier. To my mind his response to Rollins's reappearance – "He had come back too late ... [and besides] was only doing what he had always done"[41] – is much too dismissive, and indeed suggests that he had not listened very assiduously to the new work. But an earlier remark during his reflections on Rollins' meeting with Gillespie and Sonny Stitt is extremely telling:

> I think it unfortunate that Rollins felt it necessary to experiment as much as he did.[42]

To be sure, we all have to move on, and that is perhaps especially true of artists: Miles Davis's observation, "All my old records sound funny to me,"[43] is one to admire rather than question, even though he's referring *inter alia* to such albums as **Kind Of Blue** and **Porgy And Bess.** But Davis not only possessed an iron will and great courage, as I noted in Part One: he always knew exactly what he wanted to do musically at any given stage, and he also founded his every change of direction on a superb, regularly-firing rhythm section. To observe that this was not true of early 60s Rollins is not in the least to denigrate the excellent work of Hall, Hancock, McCurdy, Cranshaw, Izenon and all the other estimable musicians who worked with him during this period, but to suggest that the tenorist had not observed Clausewitz's First Principle, that of making his base secure.[44] For the Davis of the 60s Hancock, Carter and Tony Williams were his enabling constant; Rollins's rhythm-section conception was protean.

That has a positive and indeed courageous side: Rollins was at root searching for the ultimate context for his music. It is just that he did not find it – hence the continuing pick 'n' mix formations which characterised his work with Impulse! and in concert. He never achieved "the lock-down thing"[45] that he had enjoyed with Max Roach – where soloist and sidemen seem to operate as seamless extensions of each other. This might have mattered less if there were not now a tenor-led group which raised that kind of symbiosis to a newly sublime level: John Coltrane's Quartet with McCoy Tyner, Jimmy Garrison and Elvin Jones.

Although this is not the place to dwell for any length of time on that magnificent outfit, I would like to make three observations. First, not unlike the Modern Jazz Quartet in this one respect, it was a *collective*. Although the four individual members were astounding musicians, their individual contributions counted for less than the aggregate performance. The resultant group empathy and weight of sound are astonishing, and if I personally do not think its achievement superior to the sort of integration that so distinguished Davis's quintets or Peterson's trios, let there be no doubt that this was different in both kind and ethos. The key lay in the subsuming of individual virtuosity: personal expression, though of course an (invariably awesome) ingredient, ultimately mattered less than a plural oneness.

A succinct summary of that last paragraph would be that the Coltrane Quartet was greater than the sum of its parts. That cannot be said of any Rollins group of this period. It certainly was true of the Brown-Roach-Rollins band; I would argue that it also (amazingly) characterised the 'pick-up' group that cut **Saxophone Colossus** and the trio with Roach and Oscar Pettiford responsible for **The Freedom Suite**. But Rollins changed his groups' configuration too often for there to be a real chance of it happening in the 60s.

The musical ethos of the Coltrane Quartet's was underscored by the second property I want to address – an aspect of the 'politicisation' of 60s jazz that proved more durable (and aesthetically richer) than the New Thing's involvement with Black Power. By this time a significant number of jazz artists had become deeply interested in the spiritual and musical values of the East and increasingly sought to reflect them in their art. Lalo Schifrin's marvellous 1963 collaboration with Cal Tjader, **Several Shades Of Jade**, was an outstanding instance, as was the now-legendary **Music For Zen Meditation And Other Joys** recorded the following year by Tony Scott in the company of Shinichi Yuize and Hozan Yamamoto.[46] But perhaps the greatest and certainly the most sustained expression of this developing fascination with the East is to be found in Coltrane's work. Some think that his exploration of the goals and imperatives of world religions reached its peak in his highly abstract final recordings; I am not one of them. This is partly because I just don't like the records; however, the main reason is that by this time Tyner and Jones had left the group, and despite Coltrane's extreme virtuosity, the music does not have the extraordinary density of the Quartet's work. And that density, to repeat, derives from a self-subsumation in the interests of the whole, which is a definitive characteristic of Eastern spiritualism.

For some time Sonny Rollins also had been interested in oriental disciplines. During a visit to Japan in 1963 he began studying yoga on a formal basis and for five years maintained contact with his teacher, Master Oki, and with the Yoga Institute of Japan. On his return in 1968 he spent time at Oki's school in Mishima, near Mt. Fuji and commented to Ira Gitler:

> The atmosphere creates an attitude for meditation. There is a feeling of peace. Some of the students were jazz fans.[47]

This experience led him to India and an ashram, a development I explore in Part Three. The point I want to make at this juncture is that whatever the *personal* benefits Rollins may have gained from such dedicated exposure to the ways of the East – and they appear to have been considerable – the effect on his *music* was much less decisive. There is quite a lot of RCA evidence to suggest that he attempted to bring a Coltrane-like collective egalitarianism to his work; the trouble is, it seems to me, that to do so forced him to go against his natural grain as a free-wheeling, massively authoritative improviser. Coltrane found a new serenity and a new beauty through his immersion in dense group dynamics; Rollins, no matter how much he may have approved spiritually of the virtues of self-effacement, struggled to make them a cogent part of his art. It is significant that the best passage on *Oleo* on **Our Man In Jazz** is where he stretches out with all his old majesty, *sans* Don Cherry and underpinned by bass and drums; his attempts elsewhere on that session and on the meeting with Hawkins to function chiefly as an organic part of a larger whole are conspicuously less edifying.

My third and final observation seems to invite ridicule – as banal to the point of futility; arbitrary; self contradictory; invidious; or all four and more. But here goes: unlike John Coltrane, Sonny Rollins did not have McCoy Tyner. To single out the pianist may seem to fly in the face of all I've said about the Coltrane Quartet's ethos; nevertheless, I think it throws significant light on Rollins's work of this vintage. Many years later he and Tyner joined on **The Milestone Jazz All Stars In Concert**[48], which on occasion offers a poignant demonstration of what might have been. Tyner was of course utterly committed to

Coltrane's music until the tenorist went in a direction he did not feel able to follow, and it would be frivolous in the extreme to imagine that Rollins could have hired him even if he'd wanted to. What I *am* suggesting is that Rollins would have benefitted enormously from some such partnership at this time. For Tyner was not just a great pianist but also an orchestral thinker of marked depth and originality.[49] He soon became in effect Coltrane's musical director, and there is no doubt that many of the tenorist's triumphs hinged on Tyner's multiple talents, not least his prodigious work-rate and stamina.

Coltrane wasn't the only tenorist who drew deep inspiration and succour from a major musical brain who also played magnificent piano. The mid 60s marked the beginning of Stan Getz's momentous association with Chick Corea. In March 1967 they cut **Sweet Rain,** and a few years later Getz would commission an entire new book from Corea to mark his re-appearance after a two-year rest: the result was the no less seminal **Captain Marvel.**[50]

All that is not to suggest that Rollins was rather pitifully left out in the cold: he remained a magnificent improviser when the force was with him, and neither Coltrane nor Getz could have conceived (let alone executed) performances such as the long versions of *Now's The Time, Trav'lin Light* and *52nd Street Theme*. But it does perhaps point to why his art was somewhat indeterminate: when the force was *not* with him, there was no one of similar status and quality to supply it. That remained the case when he signed to Impulse! in 1965.

Lest that last sentence imply a lukewarm response to the four albums Rollins cut for the company, I should say at once that two of them are in the main superb and thirty years on the other two remain absorbing. The first, **There Will Never Be Another You,** is something of a discographical oddity: recorded on June 17, 1965 it was not released officially until 1978[51], although bootleg versions were available long before. It preserves a concert given at

NYC's Museum of Modern Art, where Rollins the experimentalist is well in evidence: he used two drummers (Higgins and Mickey Roker) and in *Mademoiselle De Paris* surpassed himself in eccentric choice of material. At the same time the music is unflaggingly high-spirited, and it also commemorates a reunion with the great Tommy Flanagan. The title track and *To A Wild Rose* are excellent, and an invigorating *Three Little Words* abounds in humour and invention.

A month later Bob Thiele welcomed Rollins into his studio to record **On Impulse!**. The title was deftly welcoming; more important, the date was Rollins's first classic quartet album (piano, bass and drums) since his sabbatical. It reunited him with Ray Bryant in a group completed by Roker and Walter Booker, and although the opening *On Green Dolphin Street* leaves something to be desired (Rollins seems out of sorts, his tone bleary and smudged), the remaining four tracks are inspired. The tenorist is not quite at his best on *Everything Happens To Me*, but his stringent examination of the tune contains moments of rhapsodic trenchancy, and Bryant is superb both as feed and in solo.

In my view the remaining three tracks – Side Two of the original LP issue – comprise Rollins's best work since his return. *Hold 'Em Joe* is a rollicking calypso: if not quite in the class of the 1956 *St. Thomas*, its swaggering élan is a heartening return to Rollins's jazz roots. *Blue Room* is piquant and sardonic by turns, beautifully orchestrated by Bryant's stealthy feeding; and *Three Little Words* is simply one of the tenorist's greatest performances – "smoothly amazing" is Philip Larkin's perfect summary.[52] Rollins begins in apparently flippant mood, slapping the tune's trifling phrases around as if cuffing an errant child, but his reading rapidly gathers force, urgently re-casting melody and harmony. As he gathers full steam Bryant lays out, enabling Rollins to feed off Booker and Roker with the kind of coruscating brilliance that ennobles his best 50s work; an extended coda confirms the depth of structural exploration amidst reminders of that initially subversive approach. Tonally versatile too – new effects are allied to that old rasping sonorousness – *Three Little Words* is endlessly stimulating, a triumphant climax to an essential album.

Six months later came **Alfie,** which prompts a brief confessional digression. The record had always disappointed me, and I reviewed its 1997 CD reissue in commensurately lukewarm terms. I argued that the engagement of Oliver Nelson was mistaken, that Phil Woods was wasted, pianist Roger Kellaway was not really in tune with the tenorist's style, and that while the two treatments of the title tune were interesting to compare, one needed to go to the JVC album **Sonny Rollins In Japan** to discover what he could *really* do with the tune. "A missed opportunity" was my concluding judgment.[53]

I like to believe my review was not a lazy one, but having re-explored the music for the purposes of this book, I do think it was seriously awry. The only excuse I can offer outside human fallibility is that I have never cared for the film itself – an archly raffish sub-morality tale that has dated badly and to whose eponymous anti-hero's antics Nat Hentoff does far too much honour, describing them in the album's notes as "the involuntary education of a hipster." That said, I confused celluloid with vinyl, and that won't do.[54]

The main title is a standard AABA 32-bar line – a swaggering, very singable motif with the B-modulation scored by Oliver Nelson. However, in every respect bar that purely structural one, *Alfie's Theme* is a *blues*. By the time Rollins re-enters, brief but splendid solos by Kellaway and guitarist Kenny Burrell have established an irresistible blues-drenched groove which the tenorist builds on with thrilling remorselessness. He takes seven choruses whose effect is almost identical to twenty-eight seamless blues choruses, as authentic as *Mambo Bounce* and *Strode Rode.* Kellaway gives stirring support early and late, but for the core Rollins relies on just Booker and drummer Frankie Dunlop (both superb).

If the rest of the album's music does not quite emulate that opening splendour, it would be wrong to call it anti-climactic. The very next track, *He's Younger Than You Are,* offers a startling contrast. Nelson's delicately incisive chart and perfectly judged commentary from Woods and Kellaway enhance some of Rollins's most tender work on record. The voluptuous piquancy of his sound is a special delight, recalling *You Don't Know What Love Is* on **Saxophone Colossus**; the same varied fullness also distinguishes *On Impulse* and *Little Malcolm Loves His Dad.* And although Nelson's orchestra is more in evidence on the differently-angled reprise of the main title, the pile-driving swing is unaltered, and Rollins takes the opportunity to essay some fresh tonal effects. (Incidentally, on the new 20-bit reissue one can frequently hear the tenorist's fingering – not an important feature, maybe, but an intriguing bonus.)

In all, **Alfie** is a distinguished work, and if my recognition of that has been woefully belated, at least I got the point in the end. However, I haven't yet managed a similar *volte-face* over its Impulse! successor. **East Broadway Rundown** was Rollins's last album for the company; as might be deduced from his hiring Jimmy Garrison and Elvin Jones it represents, along with the RCA **Our Man In Jazz,** his most concerted attempt to explore avant-garde territory. Enthusiasts of the genre responded very favourably to its release, as did more than a few for whom the New Thing was normally anathema. The consensus was that Rollins had brilliantly engaged the freedom of the new music while honouring more conservative values such as swing, recognisable melody and the ability to play in tune. I am not so sanguine.

The album is very much 'one of two halves', a characteristic possibly more obvious on the original two-sided LP than on its present CD configuration. The title track adds Freddie Hubbard for a quartet performance that begins as a blues but then goes 'outside', a development the trumpeter delighted in:

> … soon all three of us were moving out of the chords. It was beautiful, not having a piano, because that way we were not only freer harmonically but we were also not confined by the usual twelve-bar structure.[55]

Hubbard plays as well as that enthusiasm might indicate, but I am far from convinced that Rollins himself benefits from not being structurally "confined". The theme (if one can call it that) is vaguely reminiscent of his *Pent-Up House*, but reductivised and perfunctory. Rollins begins (as he often does) with a succession of simple phrases, but the rest of this first solo suggests not so much a man who has lost his way as one unsure where he was going in the first place. This is to an extent camouflaged by Garrison's wall-of-sound accompaniment and his subsequent solo, a masterpiece that lends the music sorely-needed shape and body. Jones then takes over for a customarily awesome display, but in the midst of this separate magnificence from Coltrane's men one increasingly wonders about Rollins's place and purpose. A hypnotic single-note ostinato figure from Garrison eventually ushers in tenor and trumpet for a rather messy duet re-examining the theme, before Rollins embarks on his second substantial contribution.

The passage in question is admittedly riveting – Rollins's only attempt to explore at length the 'squeaking' properties of the instrument in the way that Shepp, Coltrane and Albert Ayler pioneered. But once again I do not find it entirely convincing – mainly because I detect in Rollins himself a lack of complete conviction: he seems to vacillate between the committed and the subversive. As one has long come to expect from the tenorist, there is considerable humour throughout, but on this occasion it is uneasy and inconsistent – at one moment mordant and cryptic, at another almost satirical, as in his sudden insertion during a furiously 'free' passage of a simple triad played as a curtailed arpeggio. Another reading of that moment might posit a now-unhappy *recourse* to that most basic of musical figures: the deliberate jettisoning of form had led to him being stranded and he needed that fundamental navigational aid.

As noted, Hubbard acquits himself very well, and it is no fault of his that the rest of the album, without him, is more successful. *Blessing In Disguise* is another Rollins composition; though in fact a sixteen-bar line, like *Alfie's Theme* it impresses as an authentic blues, and does so in a way that casts further retrospective doubt on the deconstructionist *East Broadway Rundown*. In addition Rollins's tone is, to my ears at least, altogether more pleasing here, characterised by a virility and smoothness that drew this expert analysis from the absent Hubbard:

> Some of the quality of [Sonny's] tone is due to the strength of his body. He knows how to get the right amount of air into his horn and he has the strength to keep it coming and to control it. He always had a deep sound, and he learned how to perfect that depth of sound all over the instrument, from top to bottom. Many tenor players, when they play deep in the lower register, sound as if they're growling. Not Sonny.[56]

Rollins's solos are separated by a lyrical and adventurous outing from Garrison, and the tenorist also seems entirely at one with Jones (which as Ronald Atkins and others have observed has not always been the case). Not the least felicity of *Blessing In Disguise* is the ingenious way in which it segues into *We Kiss In A Shadow*. Another apparently 'odd-ball' choice – I know of no other reading in the entire jazz canon – this selection from *The King And I* emerges as pure Rollins, Romantic tenderness offset by ironic detachment.

East Broadway Rundown is one of friend and critic Michael Tucker's "favourite recordings",[57] and I can understand why. It has prodigious energy; it is courageous and full of enterprise; there is always a great deal going on, and one hears new things with each playing. But in the end the title track stumps me. Paradoxically, while it is unquestionably an important performance, it is also an inconsequential one. There is nothing quite like it anywhere else in the tenorist's *oeuvre*; yet that is significant in another way, in that Rollins never returned to such turbulent waters: the inference is that he had no desire to.

Although it lasted less than two years and spawned just four albums, Rollins's association with Impulse! was important to him.[58] But it was not a watershed: he was, it would seem, no clearer by 1966 about what was the best or ultimate context for his art than he had been in 1964. With hindsight the period turned out to be just the first stage of a process identified in 1984 by Gary Giddins:

> Rollins had to make his own way through the excesses of freedom, fusion and tradition [before resolving] a host of ambivalences.[59]

Another way of putting it – not too unkindly, I hope – is that digesting the "excesses of freedom" was a phase in Rollins's development rather than the decisive epiphany that he and others had hoped for on his re-emergence, and that he needed another period of woodshedding. He did not formally retire this time: *Down Beat* issues of the period include references to various live gigs, some of which have since appeared on record. But it would be six years before he saw the inside of a recording studio again – a period which just happened to coincide with "jazz's worst slump in its fifty years of recorded history."

Notes

1 Hugh Brogan, *The Pelican History of the United States* (Harmondsworth: Penguin, 1986), 633.

2 Alistair Cooke had this to say about those words in his "Epilogue: Vietnam" to *Talk About America* (Bodley Head, 1968, 252), also broadcast as a *Letter From America* on BBC Radio 4 on 24 March, 1968: "This is fine to read but fatal to act on. It may be the wish of a strong nation to do this, but in reality it will not support any friend or fight any foe, or support the burden, say, of a civil war in its own land, in order to rush to the aid of forty-three foes. Vietnam, I fear, is the price of the Kennedy Inaugural." It will be evident from what follows in the main text that I share his interpretation.

3 Sleeve essay to **Swing Trumpet Kings**, Verve 2-CD 533 263-2.

4 This was the time when a no-concessions jazz album (Stan Getz & Charlie Byrd's **Jazz Samba**) spent over seventy weeks on *BillBoard's* best-sellers chart, including several weeks at #1.

5 Charles Fox's words, which "on reflection" in 1969 Philip Larkin thought - and I agree with him - "a very curious opinion indeed" (*All What Jazz*, 243).

6 Shepp's latter-day career is an exemplary case in point. After what many regard as a *succés fou* in the 1960s, Shepp reverted to earlier idioms, becoming an accomplished (though markedly unoriginal) practitioner of hard bop.

7 Gitler, *Swing To Bop*, 162.

8 Mike Hennessey, 'An Interview With Oscar Peterson', *Gallery*, June 1976, 39.

9 See above, pages 18 and 26.

10 It was also dishonest, or at the very least inconsistent: Shepp worked regularly with two white musicians, Charlie Haden and Roswell Rudd.

11 See above, pages 62-63. See also Alistair Horne, 'The Year The World Turned', *The Times*, Wednesday December 31, 1997.

12 Quoted in *All What Jazz*, 262.

13 Goldberg, *Jazz Masters Of The Fifties*, 87.

14 Rollins has however remarked: "I like hard physical work," and he did take a number of menial jobs during his sabbatical, almost certainly for therapeutic rather than financial reasons.

15 The contract with RCA was for $80,000 - a prodigious amount for a jazz musician in those days. For further comments on the company's deal and policy with Rollins, see below, pages 83-84.

16 For some reason these sides were not issued in the USA until 1992.

17 Goldberg, 88.

18 Barry McRae, *The Jazz Cataclysm* (Letchworth: Aldine, 1967), 93-95, and see also *Jazz Journal*, xviii / 3 (1965), 6-7; Williams, *The Jazz Tradition*, 191-2 and see also *Jazz Journal*, xix / 7 (1966), 24-26; Brian Priestley, *Jazz: The Essential Companion*, 427; Collier, *The Making Of Jazz*, 452.

19 In fact, the 6-CD set's annotation does delete the question mark throughout; the original LP issues and the French RCA 2-LP reissue I possess retain it. So does the actual song *What's New?* – and since that is not amongst the album's selections, **What's New** might seem the better choice and indeed the better musical 'signal'. That said, I have decided to stick throughout to the original issue's typography.

20 Loren Schoenberg, *The Complete RCA Recordings of Sonny Rollins*; essay accompanying the 6-CD set analysed in the main text. NYC: BMG Music, 1997, 17-18. Jim Hall's final sentence quoted here is especially shrewd, and I return to it on page 64.

21 *Jazz Journal International*, l /4 (1997), 40.

22 Schoenberg, 20-21.

23 *Ibid*, 21.

24 *Ibid*, 20.

25 On the Verve album **Didn't We**, SVLP 9248 (UK LP issue). The album has yet to be reissued on CD.

26 Gene Lees, *Oscar Peterson: The Will To Swing* (Toronto: Lester & Orpen Dennys, 1988), 251.

27 Preserved on **The Complete Concert 1964** (recorded at the Lincoln Centre's Philharmonic Hall); Columbia Sony 471246-2.

28 See Note 56, Part One.

29 *Jazz Journal International*, l /11 (1997), 37.

30 On Moon 053-2 & 054-2.

31 Schoenberg, 24.

32 *Ibid*, 25.

33 A wry reflection offered by Riverside's then owner, Orrin Keepnews; it appears in his 'Reissue Producer's Note'

accompanying Schoenberg's essay for the RCA 6-CD set, 16.

34 Schoenberg, 21.

35 *Ibid*, 23.

36 *Jazz Journal International*, l /11 (1997), 38.

37 Amazingly, the 1997 6-CD represents the first USA issue of this unique performance.

38 *Jazz Journal International*, l /11 (1997), 38.

39 Gordon Kopulos, 'Needed Now: Sonny Rollins', *Down Beat* xxxviii / 13 (1971) 12-13 & 30.

40 *The Guardian*, January 23, 1968.

41 *The Making of Jazz*, 452.

42 *Ibid*, 452.

43 Leonard Feather, 'Miles', *From Satchmo To Miles* (London: Quartet, 1974), 227.

44 Clausewitz was talking about war, not music, but the analogy still serves.

45 The phrase is Oscar Peterson's, in reference to his trios with Ray Brown & Herb Ellis and Brown & Ray Thigpen. See Lees, *The Will To Swing*, 128.

46 Verve has recently reissued both albums; Schifrin-Tjader is on 314 537 083-2, Scott on 314 521 444-2.

47 Ira Gitler, 'Sonny Rollins: Music Is An Open Sky', *Down Beat*, xxxvi / 11 (1969), 18-19.

48 Recorded September & October 1978, and to be found on Milestone M-55006. The music is discussed in detail in Part Three.

49 This was evident from his first trio recordings for Impulse - **Inception, Night of Ballads And Blues** and perhaps especially **Reaching Forth** and **Plays Ellington** – and confirmed by his writing (in harness with Eric Dolphy) for Coltrane's **Africa/Brass**. And in the 1990s his orchestral gifts were sumptuously resurrected in big band recordings for the Birdology label – **The Turning Point** and **Journey** (513 163-2 & 519 941-2).

50 In passing, the Getz-Corea concert at the Royal Festival Hall in November 1967 (with Walter Booker and Roy Haynes) remains one of the greatest gigs I have attended. There is no evidence that it was recorded.

51 By ABC Records; Impulse! A 9349.

52 *All What Jazz*, 153.

53 *Jazz Journal International*, l / 8 (1997), 38.

54 One of the pleasures of such a radical change of mind is the chance to applaud Paramount's initiative. The company bankrolled the movie on the assumption that it would be a box-office hit (which it duly proved), so it was both brave and imaginative to commission a jazz musician to write the score. Although I still don't like the film much, I am very pleased it was so successful.

55 On the sleeve to **East Broadway Rundown,** Impulse! 11612.

56 *Ibid.*

57 *Jazz Journal International* il /2 (1996), 19.

58 Those with a liking for 'sampler' or 'Best of ...' packages are warmly directed to a 1997 medium-price CD on Priceless 98762 (an imprint of GRP Records). It collects *Alfie's Theme*; *We Kiss In A Shadow* and *Blessing in Disguise* from **East Broadway Rundown**; and all of **On Impulse!** bar *On Green Dolphin Street.*

59 Gary Giddins, *Rhythm-a-ning* (New York: Oxford University Press, 1986), 268-9.

HORN CULTURE: The 1970s and beyond

For several years Rollins has been moving in the direction of a music that suggests the fires of blessed inspiration with none of the penalties.... (He) was never comfortable with the lavish disclosures of self, the musical glossolalia, the narcissism let loose in the wake of Coltrane.

Gary Giddins, 1984[1]

If the reasons for Rollins's first sabbatical were complex and multiple – a mixture of pressure, fatigue and artistic doubt – then his second retirement was a simpler matter. It was born of frustration.

The most immediate symptom was the state of his own art. By the mid-60s he was no more certain about where he should concentrate his energies than he had been in 1959. It would not be fair to label the five years that began with **The Bridge** and culminated in **East Broadway Rundown** 'anti-climactic': Rollins produced too many memorable performances for that to stand up. They do, however, betray a governing lack of ease. Unsure whether to refine what he had already accomplished or to experiment with increased boldness, Rollins cast around in near-febrile fashion for backing musicians, material, tonal and stylistic approach, even markets. Compared to the work of Getz or Gillespie his response to the bossa nova was a dilettante flirtation; so, too, was his dalliance with avant-gardists Don Cherry and Paul Bley. His forays into that latter territory now seem muted, even dispiriting: one has the impression that he genuflected to the avant garde simply because it was there, not because its innovations truly convinced or enabled him. By the end of 1966 his residual diffidence had resurfaced: it was again time to re-think, and above all to stay away from the studio.

But there was more to this frustration than personal angst. For it cannot possibly have escaped Rollins – always the most astute of musical observers – that jazz was in a very bad way. Clubs were folding by the month; the jazz record business was shrinking equally fast; the customers were increasingly dissatisfied and growing ever-fewer in number. On both sides of the Atlantic the writing was on the wall, and it was thrown into even starker relief on July 17, 1967, when John Coltrane died, aged just forty.

Coltrane was in many fundamental respects an extreme musician, and his music prompted commensurately extreme reactions – from adulation to detestation, and all points in between. Nevertheless, there is little doubt that he was the most charismatic and influential jazzman of the period – more so than even Miles Davis, let alone Rollins himself. In 1965 Coltrane had won four separate categories in the "Readers' Poll" conducted by *Down Beat*; moreover, each victory – Hall of Fame, Jazzman of the Year, Tenor Saxophone and Record of the Year – was by a street.[2] And while that winning record – **A Love Supreme** – marked the point of no return for more than a few listeners, his work still attracted huge acclaim from his many remaining acolytes.[3] Moreover, it continued to compel even where it most unsatisfied, exemplified in the writings of that apparently beyond-the-pale reactionary Philip Larkin.

In June 1962 Larkin had written, "Coltrane's records are paradoxically nearly always both interesting and boring, and I certainly find myself listening to them in preference to many a less adventurous set."[4] His interest never waned even if his grudging pleasure vanished; so, although he found one Coltrane album "the most astounding piece of ugliness I have ever heard" and observed of another "Soloists appear and submerge like *Titanic* passengers", he reviewed Coltrane's every record.[5] That could be seen as dry conscientiousness or even tawdry venality; I believe the truth to be more edifying.

Larkin as jazz critic is chiefly famous (many would say notorious) for his *Introduction* to *All What Jazz*. This is not the place for a detailed analysis of the fascinating discrepancy between that preludial essay's celebrated attack on Modernism and the *Daily Telegraph* columns it prefaces.[6] Nor will I dwell on his confessed meretriciousness –

> In literature, I understood, there were several old whores who had grown old in the reviewing game by praising everything, and I planned to be their jazz equivalent.[7]

– other than to nail it as wittily disingenuous: as his great friend Kingsley Amis pointed out, writing solely for money is

> A uniquely, odiously painful activity: not really worth the money, in fact.[8]

I will instead stick to simple arithmetic. The main text of *All What Jazz* collects 126 columns written monthly over eleven years between February 1961 and December 1971. They comprise over 900 record reviews plus some 30 book & periodical reviews.[9] No virtue in mere numbers, it could be said: plenty of people have written a great deal of rubbish. Agreed; what makes those figures truly imposing is the quality of insight that complements them. It happens that I own or know well approximately 400 of the records he covers. Divergence of taste and so forth duly admitted, the reviews are invariably cogent and more often than not decisively illuminating. Even more striking – as I trust has been evident in examples quoted already, including of course his references to Rollins – his single-sentence summaries of this record or that artist are masterly not only in their economy but in their incisiveness.

Quantitatively and qualitatively those 126 columns severely undermine, if not destroy, the *Introduction*'s polemic. Its portrait of Larkin-as-old-jazz-whore is a variant of the "winning curmudgeon" persona deftly identified by Joseph Epstein[10], and it won't wash. Nobody who was "patently unfitted" to write about jazz records or most of whose listening resembled a "nightmare"[11] could have done such a stint, and one must find Larkin happily guilty of being motivated by love or at the very least deep interest.

However, there is no doubt that from around 1968 the columns start to evince disenchantment, even bad temper. (It is worth stressing that the *Introduction* itself was written in that year.) One notices an increasingly predominant focus on pre-war jazz and reissues, and his observations on 'modern' jazz are more obviously waspish than characterised his earlier judgments.[12] In all, it is in retrospect no surprise that he called it a day at the end of 1971 or to find him reflecting in the *Footnote To The Second Edition*, written in 1984: "I'm sure I was right [to stop when I did]."[13]

And yet – and this is why I've devoted nearly a thousand words to him – history has vindicated Larkin's Goldwynesque "include me out" exit. Far from being the reactionary maverick he so enjoyed fabricating, Larkin articulated better than anyone else I have read the growing anxiety experienced by jazz enthusiasts of almost all persuasions. They (and Sonny Rollins was assuredly one of their number) noted with alarm that what only a few years ago had been a music of affirmation, earthy power and communicative zeal was in serious danger of becoming a narcissistic dead end.

In sum: Larkin's *Record Diary* (*All What Jazz*'s resonant sub-title) dramatised the 60s demise of jazz as 'good time music' while also decisively pin-pointing its lack of direction. And he was at his most acute – one gratuitous adjective aside – in his observations of August 1967:

> I regret Coltrane's death, as I regret the death of any man, but I can't conceal the fact that it leaves in jazz a vast, a blessed silence.[14]

"Blessed" is a value judgment that many will (angrily) reject; the rest approaches unanswerable fact. Coltrane's sudden demise was not just immensely sad: it threw jazz into a chaotic limbo, accelerating (to repeat) the "worst slump in its fifty years of recorded history." [15]

But was jazz itself entirely to blame? The same writer offers a cogently guarded answer, citing "post-avant garde shock and the advent of rock" as twin causes.[16] I would simply add that the two were in some respects intimately connected.

Despite the thrust of my argument thus far, I am well aware that history has more than vindicated the leading figures of the 60s avant garde. I have already had my say about Archie Shepp, and on the subject of Albert Ayler I'll pass, but the achievements of Cecil Taylor, Ornette Coleman and John Coltrane are beyond dispute. Moreover, Coleman and Taylor continue to produce stirring, often electrifying work, and while Coltrane has been dead these thirty years, his *oeuvre* grows in stature and indeed popularity: he is amongst the bigger sellers of the CD-revivified jazz market. But not even its most ardent champion could claim that this music was any *fun*. Its chief ingredients were sheer difficulty, a predilection for unvaried *fortissimo* and a supercilious disdain for vulgar 'entertainment'; the recipe was additionally over-egged via a remorseless solemnity. Many committed and intrepid *aficionados* found such fare indigestible: small wonder that it was rejected by any and all diners seeking an undemandingly enjoyable evening out.

Rock *was* fun; by now it was also big business on a scale that would have seemed unimaginable ten years before. The second half of the 50s had seen a prodigious increase in record sales, from $82 million in 1954 to $521 million in 1960; by the mid-60s those statistics had been dwarfed as rock conquered the globe. The key players in this staggeringly rapid process were Elvis Presley and the Beatles.

No less a figure than Leonard Bernstein has called Presley "the greatest cultural force in the twentieth century."[17] When he burst onto the scene in 1956 'Elvis the Pelvis' was a talent as shocking for some as he was exciting for others, full of a raw power whose sexuality was palpable. He drew on the separate-yet-linked traditions of hillbilly music and the blues, a potent combination made all the more heady by a voice at once true and husky and a rhythmic flair that no other mass-selling artist has ever approached. To an America gripped by the Cold War and for which McCarthyism was still an issue, Presley was – to cite one of his more exhilarating songs – 'Trouble'. What he communicated and seemed to stand for struck many as not only alarming but indecent to the point of un-Americanness. Thus in 1958 one finds a critic writing to a Senate sub-committee on delinquency –

> Elvis Presley is a symbol . . (and) a dangerous one. His strip-tease antics threaten to rock 'n' roll the juvenile world into open revolt against society. The gangster of tomorrow is the Elvis Presley type today.[18]

- and a psychiatrist intoning in the *New York Times*

> Rock 'n' roll is a communicable disease ... a cannibalistic and tribalistic kind of music.[19]

To read all that now, twenty-plus years after Presley's death, is both comic and sad. For we all know what happened next, to Presley in particular and such "dangerous" youth culture in general. In the words of James T. Patterson:

> Rock 'n' roll, like much else in the United States, quickly became commodified – a vital part of the thriving culture of consumption.[20]

Presley remained youth-oriented and 'Trouble' for another year or so, during which time he had a string of hits mining further that raunchy power – e.g. *Jailhouse Rock, I Got Stung, Big Hunk*

Of Love and *Hard-Headed Woman*. Yet even while America and Britain's young were rocking and rolling to such joyous, quasi-anarchic sounds, a softening-up process was going on. Colonel Tom Parker, Presley's egregious manager, had already determined that Elvis would become an all-round family entertainer, motivated by those twin (indeed symbiotic) forces, small-town conservative propriety and money-lust. Thus in 1958 Presley went into the army, was fashioned into the model, modestly dutiful soldier, and by the time he was de-mobbed, middle America – and indeed middle-*aged* America – had taken him to their hearts. Parker's long-term plan stream-rollered into action, powered by records that were tame, even unctuous, when set beside the 'old' Elvis and by conveyor-belt movies of increasingly inane lousiness. Parker (and presumably Presley too) cried all the way to the bank: people still flocked in their millions to the record stores and the cinemas. It was a lesson not lost on a Liverpudlian then in his late twenties, Brian Epstein.

Until his sudden death in 1967 Epstein managed a number of highly successful rock & pop acts, amongst them Gerry and the Pacemakers, Billy J. Kramer and Cilla Black. But the Beatles were of course his main 'creation'.* When he heard the group at the now-legendary Cavern Club in Liverpool, Epstein was captivated not so much by their act as by the potential he perceived, and he set about maximising it. He fired drummer Pete Best, replacing him with Ringo Starr; he smartened up their wardrobe and stage presentation; he arranged a contract with EMI's Parlophone label. Within two years he had transformed their raw energy and cheerily *gamin* appeal into the most successful outfit in the history of popular entertainment.

The key to the Beatles was that they appealed to people of *all* age groups, classes and musical tastes. Few will need reminding that they took the teenage (and younger) market by storm in spectacular fashion. Just months after their first hit in the autumn of 1962 (the modestly successful *Love Me Do*) 'Beatlemania'

* The Frankenstein connotations are deliberate on my part.[21]

consumed Britain, and a similarly saturative wave would sweep America before 1963 was out. But like the 'remodelled' Presley – only more so – they captivated the middle-aged as well, and even the old; unlike Presley, they also elicited accolades from the musical intelligentsia. Moreover, they were soon the darlings of the City: their colossal appeal occasioned commensurate global sales, and in 1964 each was awarded the MBE for services to exports. A number of Blimpish figures returned their gongs in disgust as a result, but that seemed only to increase the group's charm. Not only was British pop all the rage in the USA: for the first time since the inception of rock 'n' roll, trends and styles were being determined in the UK. America cloned its own version of the Beatles – the Monkees, whose records and TV series were immensely popular on both sides of the Atlantic; even the continued successes of the Motown stable could not stem the tide of influence. The capital of England was about to become known as 'Swinging London'; a culture that young and old alike could enjoy and share was booming. It was all down to the 'Fab Four': Epstein's carefully sanitized creature was *everyone*'s favourite group.[22]

To this day I find the speed with which rock took over the Establishment spookily amazing. Originally an expression of pent-up youthful energy underscored by an iconoclasm no less healthy for being simplistic, rock had by the mid-60s become not only socially acceptable but an authentic political force. By that I mean something altogether more significant than the award by Harold Wilson's Government of those MBEs or pop stars endorsing Presidential candidates. Rock was now an *ideology*, and millions fell over themselves to embrace it. In the first place, it was good clean family fun – a quality 'officially' codified in 1967 when BBC's Radio One took up the mantle of the now-defunct pirate stations. Second, a liking for rock was proof that you were a card-carrying member of the caring classes, a sensitive and right-thinking human being. 'Protest pop' was a major feature of 1965 and before long there came Flower Power, the Maharishi and *All You Need Is Love*. By the end of the decade, half a million people would be at Woodstock to sing hymns of praise to rock-as-icon.

The fact that it's easy to be rude about 60s rock doesn't make it any less pleasurable or necessary to be so. Compared to their counterparts of today, rock musicians were far less proficient; many were indeed comically awful, including some global luminaries of the genre. Its sense of form was puny, its harmonies feeble and its lyrics fatuous. Moreover, rock had a pretentiousness quite foreign to its 50s origins – a property that its audience was all too willing to connive at: how else explain the success in 1965 of Barry McGuire's cretinously apocalyptic *Eve of Destruction* or the widespread belief that the nasal ramblings of Bob Dylan were statements of genius? Both musically and politically rock was almost unrelievedly puerile – and its vast acceptance by people of all ages and levels of intelligence signalled a comprehensive dumbing-down as sterile as depressing.

As an art form distinguished for its idealism and integrity, jazz might have been able to stem this growing reductivism if it had been in better shape and able to compete musically. But the New Thing and all its knock-on consequences put paid to any such possibility. In 1967 Miles Davis observed darkly, "Twenty years ago jazz was pop music. Today it has only a small proportion of the public on its side."[23] Too many jazzmen had turned their back on the audience, on the need to keep the foot engaged as well as the brain, and on Lester Young's ultimate court of appeal, "Can you sing me a song?"[24] Rock may have been reductive, and in its own way it was every bit as solemn as the New Wave of jazz. On the other hand, its tunes were instantly memorable and its beat, no matter how anodyne, was infectious and danceable. Many hip blacks and whites had danced to bebop and to hard bop; no one danced to the strains of the New Thing.

And so in the 60s the relationship between jazz and popular music, for so long a companionable and often symbiotic one, reduced to a battle between beetle-browed elitism in one corner and the Beatles in the other. It was no contest, and even the most glamorous and apparently immune jazz stars suffered as a result. In August 1968 bassist Dave Holland replaced Ron Carter in the

Miles Davis Quintet and immediately found out how prescient were the just-quoted words of his new boss:

> We played a lot of clubs where there were sort of thirty or forty people in the audience in a night. We played gigs out in San Francisco in, I think it was September of that year ... and I was amazed that so few people would come. I thought that, working with Miles, it would be a packed house every time ...[25]

If even Davis could not command large audiences, then jazz was assuredly in deep trouble. Holland reckons that this was the time when the trumpeter said to himself, ''I've got to make a change. There's got to be a change in the music'. Being Davis, he at once set about effecting that change. And while not everyone could enthuse about what it did to Davis's own music, it is I think beyond question that his initiatives did curative service to jazz.

It is a moot point just how radical those initiatives were. Rock material had already become a telling ingredient in several jazzmen's repertoire, as had the use of electronic instruments: both were regular features of Jimmy Smith's Verve records, for example. Jazz groups' use of the Fender (electric) bass was increasingly common, and not just in more 'progressive' bands: it played a key part in Bill Holman's 1967 *Concerto For Herd* for Woody Herman's orchestra, and Stan Getz used Phil Upchurch on (of all things) an album dedicated to the work of Burt Bacharach.[26] On a more exotic note, trumpeter Don Ellis formed an exciting (if occasionally near-chaotic) big band that experimented with just about everything – time signatures, rock figures, electronic instruments, amplifier distortion and loop-delay echo chambers. Even when not entirely successful, the mixture was a headily potent one: his September 1967 album **Electric Bath** remains a classic.

Nevertheless, Davis gave these new trends decisive momentum. In 1968 he had composed *Stuff*, a rock-beat based piece that occupied well over half a side of the LP **Miles In The**

Sky. Though not the album's most aesthetically satisfying track – *Black Comedy* is far superior – *Stuff* is nevertheless the most interesting, if only as a taste of things to come. Ian Carr's summary is unimprovable:

> (Davis) does not sound as magnificently confident as he does on *Black Comedy*, but somehow the very tentativeness of his playing gives it more weight; we can sense his groping for a way into a new musical area.[27]

"Tentativeness" and "groping" confirm Dave Holland's inference that Davis was already committed to the search for a new land. And if the trumpeter's response to the siren call of rock was tinged with an if-you-can't beat-'em-join-'em desperation, then his first full-blown incursion into such territory, made in February 1969, was an aesthetic and commercial event of the first order.

In terms of personal taste, **In A Silent Way** comes a fair way down the list of my favourite Davis albums. But I would gladly concede that, with the exception of **Miles Ahead** and **Kind of Blue**, it is his most important. Unusually, he was very excited about it himself, seeing it as a decisive breakthrough. As Ian Carr has pointed out, Davis's movement towards this kind of music had been launched some five years before by the track *Eighty One* on **ESP**, and its eventual fruition must have tasted sweet indeed. Buoyed up by this almost boyish enthusiasm, Davis "fell in love with the trumpet all over again" and embarked on one of the happiest periods of his career.[28]

Davis's renascence was crucial in a wider sense too. For all the quality of his 60s work, it had been some time since he was regarded as the chief prophet of jazz; now he had once more given a decisive lead. Some of the exciting developments that ensued grew almost literally out **In A Silent Way**. All three pianists on the date would soon have seminal accomplishments to their credit. Chick Corea went on to found the influential group Return To Forever; Joe Zawinul became a founder member of the even more influential – and hugely popular – Weather Report; Herbie Hancock carved out a new career in electronics: his 1973 **Head Hunters** would prove the biggest-selling jazz record ever.

But it wasn't just Davis's immediate acolytes who benefited from his enterprise and followed his lead. In September 1969 Woody Herman, who had been dallying imaginatively with aspects of rock for a couple of years[29], cut **Heavy Exposure**, with guest appearances from rock stalwarts Donny Hathaway and Phil Upchurch. A much underrated achievement in its own right, the album also telegraphed Herman's intelligent and richly productive 70s use of rock material and devices: the *locus classicus* is perhaps **Giant Steps**, which won a Grammy. Stan Getz, returning from a two year lay-off, commissioned Chick Corea to write a whole new book for him: the result was the triumphant **Captain Marvel** of 1972.

All these developments defined or embraced the form known as *crossover* or *fusion* – a marriage between rock and jazz. It was not welcomed unanimously: many purists saw it as whoring after popularity or merely as sad confirmation that jazz no longer had the wherewithal to pursue an independent life. And as one who did welcome and enjoy fusion, I have to say that most of it (though not the records just discussed above) has dated very badly.[30] But by helping to make jazz accessible and fun again, fusion established a climate where the young were once more sympathetic to jazz.

That interest soon extended to what might be termed 'authentic' jazz, reflected by the growth in recording activity which had nothing to do with fusion music as such. In Europe MPS and Black Lion – new labels devoted essentially to mainstream jazz – prospered, and in 1969 Manfred Eicher founded Editions of Contemporary Music (ECM), a major innovation that would also prove highly successful. In America Carl Jefferson launched Concord and in 1972 Norman Granz, returning to the production business after an absence of twelve years, created Pablo. Unlike Concord, Pablo nodded occasionally in fusion's direction, but its chief *raison d'etre* was to preserve the work of those whose music Granz felt was threatened, had been ignored too long, or was just too good not to be made available to a newly-hungry jazz public.[31]

"Threatened"; "ignored too long"; "too good not be made available": all three epithets exactly apply to the Sonny Rollins of the time. And one of the happier (if indirect) results of the fusion-led recovery of jazz came about in July 1972, when Rollins entered a recording studio for the first time for over six years.

II

The return of Sonny Rollins would be a glorious event – even if he didn't want to solve any dilemmas. Because he swings.

Gordon Kopulos, 1971[32]

There is far less documentation about Rollins's 1966-72 semi-sabbatical than there is about his earlier withdrawal. He continued to tour, and like many American jazz stars at the time, he seemed to find Scandinavia a congenial place. November 1965 had found him in the company of drummer Alan Dawson and bass prodigy Niels-Henning Ørsted Pedersen for dates in Copenhagen and Stockholm recently made available as **Live In Europe '65**,[33] and three years later, by which time he had long shunned the studio, he appeared at Copenhagen's famous Cafe Montmartre. Two CDs commemorating this date – **Sonny Rollins In Denmark 1 & 2**[34] – were released in the early 90s, and their importance as the first examples of Rollins's 1967-72 work to appear on record is sufficient to transcend some fairly dire engineering.

By the time he appeared at the Cafe Montmartre Rollins's *penchant* for marathon performances was a byword: even so, *Four* surely sets a new standard, weighing in at forty-seven minutes. His sheer stamina commands respect; more important is the stunning fertility and elasticity of his lines, wedded to a profound and instinctive structural sense. The rhythm section (Pedersen again, Kenny Drew and Al 'Tootie' Heath) acquit themselves superbly, although the pianist is so poorly miked that his solo seems almost to come from another room. The rest of the fare is less monumental, and largely features a *pot pourri* of Rollins favourites: *Three Little Words* survives the comparison with the **On Impulse!** version pretty well, and there's some wonderful playing from both tenor and piano on *Sonnymoon For Two*. But arguably the most significant track is the ten-minute reading of John Coltrane's *Naima*. On one level a moving threnody to the friend who had died the previous year, it also documents, both tonally and conceptually, an indebtedness to the composer; at the same time, Rollins's muscular warmth is all his own and he swings with a natural ferocity that Coltrane never could quite emulate.

This addition to the tenorist's discography is fortunate as well as valuable, for at this time Rollins had concerns other than music. His interest in yoga* led him to India, where he joined an ashram – "a religious colony of Hindu monks and women, yoginis" – meditating and taking courses in Vedanata philosophy under the guidance of the Swami Chinmayananda. The move both reflected his disillusionment with the current musical scene and also solved it, as he revealed to Ira Gitler in 1969:

> I wanted to get with people who were genuine. I was fed up with the ratrace. The teachings stress that you have to be in the ratrace, but need not be part of it. It gave me an incentive to come back.[35]

That last remark is crucial. As I've observed already, while Rollins the man may deeply value the calming mysticism of the East, Rollins the artist needs to be involved and in charge: above all, he *wanted* an incentive to come back. On a later visit to the ashram, he confessed to Gitler: "I wasn't really ready to meditate. I had to come back to this world first." That is of a piece with a remark he made five years later to Bob Porter, when he revealed that while he liked to spend a lot of time on his farm a hundred miles north of New York, he maintained a NYC address: "This is where my business is."[36]

Another important development was his marriage to Lucille, who also became his manager and later his producer. She has wryly remarked that anyone marrying Sonny Rollins knows she must take second place to the saxophone, but the marriage has been as good and enduring, and in that Porter interview Rollins paid tribute to her decisive influence:

* See above, Part Two, 90-91

> She's a real straight arrow. She keeps me in line. Left to my own devices, I can get pretty wild.[37]

There was something else that made Rollins's gigs infrequent, or at least sporadic: economics. In his article of 1969 Ira Gitler argued that Rollins's reduced activity was down to two interlocking things: personal fees and the difficulty of finding top-class sidemen who were regularly available. Gitler commented that if earlier lay-offs had been motivated by "dissatisfaction with himself or disenchantment with the jazz scene", a key factor now was money:

> If they want Sonny Rollins, then they'll have to pay my price. If I don't get it now, when am I going to get it?[38]

Rollins was not alone in his financial militancy. Ornette Coleman took much the same attitude, as had such aforementioned orgainsations as the AACM and the JCOA. However, for reasons I've explored, 1969 was just about the worst possible year for even a top jazzman to hold out for more money than was being offered – and Rollins had aesthetic desires that doubled the problem. He wanted a permanent working group, something he had not really known since his days with Clifford Brown and Max Roach. But as Gitler observed, "Sonny cannot command the full-time services of superior sidemen because he works so sporadically."[39] Rollins was trapped in a musical Catch-22: he wanted a regular group but couldn't pay them enough, and while he remained obdurate about his worth he could not build up the necessary capital. And of course he knew that perfectly well:

> There are not that many good players around. The good ones are working. There are a lot of guys I can work with and who can work with me, but until I get a steady itinerary and offer steady work...[40]

The ellipsis dramatises the vicious circle: there was, it seemed, no way out. Until Orrin Keepnews took a hand.

Few people knew Rollins better. Keepnews was not just an erstwhile producer: he was an old and trusted friend, not least because he was likewise something of an idealistic maverick. As these remarks written in 1991 demonstrate, he understood and to some extent shared Rollins's dislike of recording:

> Despite having devoted most of my life to this medium, I am well aware of the fundamental contradiction of an essentially improvised and spontaneous music being almost invariably documented under circumstances that have no necessary connection with creativity ... As producer of two Rollins albums for Riverside Records, and much later while working with the saxophonist, it became quite clear to me that this man ... really disliked the act of making records – the kind of antipathy that once led him to tell me that "all recording is a traumatic experience."[41]

But Keepnews also knew that if Rollins was to put together enough capital to do what he professed he wanted to do artistically, he had to make records. It took a long time to persuade him, as Keepnews revealed in a 1996 essay accompanying a 2-CD compilation celebrating Rollins's quarter-century with the Milestone label:

> Back in the late Sixties, Milestone was a small New York jazz label run by me ... Sonny had not recorded since his last Impulse album in 1966, but he *was* on occasion playing odd gigs – and none could have been odder than the February 18, 1969 concert at New York's Whitney Museum in which he was one of three solo performers (the others being Jimmy Giuffre and Cecil Taylor). The small venue was sold out and somehow my promised press-list ticket wasn't there ... I told (Rollins) my sad story, he smuggled me into the concert and I ended the evening in possession of a rare prize: the always-unlisted Rollins telephone number ...
>
> For what turned out to be nearly three years of intermittent

> attempts, I never succeeded in reaching him, until the day I returned from a trip to find that Mr. Rollins had phoned – leaving a quite different call-back number. In quick sequence, I called, he informed me that he was thinking of recording again and wanted to know if I was still interested...[42]

Years later Rollins told Robert Palmer that he was still somewhat reluctant to record, but that "since it was Orrin, I stepped back in the water."[43] Despite such a happy outcome, the sentence which opens Keepnews's essay was obviously written with feeling: "In order to have a 25-year run, there must first be an opening night."

Rollins's Milestone *oeuvre* has been given a decidedly mixed press almost from the outset; I shall be examining those appraisals later, in the course of making clear my own overall opinion. But I will say now that the first four albums strike me as almost unbrokenly successful. Things got off to a highly auspicious start with the skittishly entitled **Sonny Rollins' Next Album**, a quartet session featuring the stalwart Bob Cranshaw, pianist George Cables and either Jack DeJohnette or Dave Lee on drums. The material – three originals (including a new calypso) and two standards – is a typically catholic Rollins mixture; moreover, the LP's first side documents two notable innovations.

Rollins's own *Playin' In The Yard* offered instant proof of his absorption of fusion values. The attractive theme, uncomplicatedly funky on the surface, has a suppleness of form that affords the tenorist ample scope for rhythmic subtlety, and its ten minutes also demonstrates that he had lost none of his motific virtuosity as an improviser. *Playin' In The Yard* is more r & b than disco-music (a sub-genre Rollins was to investigate later, not always with felicitous results) but it is imbued with the spirit of the dance, always a key constituent of his best music. In contrast, *Poinciana* is a passionately intense performance reminiscent of Coltrane – unsurprisingly in a way, since it marks Rollins's recorded debut on soprano sax. The tune was originally made famous by pianist Ahmad Jamal, whose spare, idiosyncratic reading influenced Miles Davis amongst others; Rollins goes in an opposite direction, milking the haunting line to the full and, fuelled by the splendid Lee, generating great power.

The remaining three tracks are perhaps less 'significant' but just as satisfying, especially as in their different ways they dramatise Rollins's jazz roots. *The Everywhere Calypso* confirms his return to Jordanesque 'good time music': warmth and humour abound, and the tune inspires an excellent solo from Cables. The modal blues *Keep Hold Of Yourself*, another Rollins original, is a gratifying reminder of Rollins the *doyen* of hard bop, while the long and exquisite reading of *Skylark* recalls *You Don't Know What Love Is* or the quartet tracks on **Tenor Madness**, even if the tenor sound retains the adjustments fashioned during the 60s.

Next Album was recorded in July 1972. For **Horn Culture,** taped over three separate sessions in 1973, Rollins added percussionist Mtume and the exciting Japanese guitarist Masuo, while Cables was replaced by Walter Davis Jr. The album was striking even before one had played a note of it. Arnold Newman's cover photograph is an unforgettable portrait of Rollins-plus-sax, squaring the circle begun nearly forty years before when a friend's analogous portrait determined Rollins's choice of career.[44] The music fully lives up to that artwork's brooding promise, describing a mélange of material and idiom similar to its predecessor. *Pictures In The Reflection Of A Golden Horn* further enshrines Rollins's love affair with the saxophone (he has even written a poem on the subject) and in its use of over-dubbing announces his excursions into electronics and hi-tech possibilities.

The latter is also a feature of Mtume's *Sais*, where Rollins plays both tenor and soprano, sometimes simultaneously. The track is replete with interest, but its twelve minutes are not always free of earnestness, and while it is a performance to be valued – some of Rollins's effects on both horns are extraordinary – it is a bit wearing at times. No such stricture attends the less ambitious but pulsating *Notes For Eddie* and *Love Man*[45]. The former is another satisfying essay in funk with tenorist and Masuo in commanding form, while the latter is another reminder of Rollins the supremo of hard bop, although there's also evidence of his more recent debt to Coltrane in some of his phrasing and harmonic options. And **Horn Culture**'s remaining two tracks are arguably the best and certainly the most graceful. *God Bless The Child* is afforded a faintly funky veneer, but Rollins explores the song's pathos to perfection in a version that I find noticeably superior to that found on **The Bridge**. In similar vein, *Good Morning Heartache* re-emphasises Rollins's affinity for the 'sing me a song' genius of Lester Young; the most enduring quality of his reading – especially during the lengthy cadenza towards the end – is its *cantabile* directness.

With the partial exception of *Sais*, then, **Horn Culture** is cheering confirmation that Rollins had rediscovered all his old confidence and extrovert command. However, something even finer was just around the corner – a session which must be ranked amongst Rollins's greatest triumphs.

Of all the jazz gigs that I wish I had caught live, the night and early morning of July 6-7 at the 1974 Montreux Jazz Festival comes high on the list, if not at the very top. The final attraction was Woody Herman's Thundering Herd.[46] However, they were not able to start playing until 3.30 because of the tumultuous reception (including three encores) afforded the previous band. That was the Sonny Rollins Sextet, featuring Cranshaw, Mtume, Masuo, Lee (now Rollins's regular drummer) and Stanley Cowell on piano, and five of their selections are preserved on **The Cutting Edge**.

The group meshes superbly from the first bar, proving the wisdom of Rollins's desire for a full-time outfit, and while the title track and *First Moves* owe a superficial debt to fusion, the governing properties are the tenorist's sense of form and improvisational logic. *The Cutting Edge* is well-named: Rollins carves great swathes out of the material in joyously savage style, and its hard-driving incisiveness sets the tone for the session. He is at his most deceptively languid on Burt Bacharach's *A House Is Not A Home*, doing little more, it seems, than play the melody; closer and repeated listening makes one aware of all kinds of subtle resonances and delicate paraphrases, beautifully supported by Cowell and Lee. Even finer is Rollins's arrangement of Edward MacDowell's *To A Wild Rose*; the melody is explored with loving care before Rollins embarks on a lengthy unaccompanied passage that unsurprisingly brought the crowd to its feet. The combination of unerring virtuosity and mellow tenderness makes the earlier reading on **There Will Never Be Another You** seem ordinary by comparison.

It is, however, the album's final track that excites most. For *Swing Low, Sweet Chariot* Rollins added Rufus Harley on bagpipes. Harley is a good tenor and soprano player (q.v.) but it is on the Scottish instrument that he has carved his particular niche in jazz. I remember a 70s club date in England where he and Rollins tore the place up with some of the most inspired improvising I have witnessed, and their re-casting of the old spiritual is no less terrific. It starts with an *a capella* duet between the horns, where Rollins hypnotically explores the tenor's drone properties in counterpoint to Harley's treble wailing.[47] Both in their phrasing and melodic ideas the two men complement each other almost uncannily before Lee and Cranshaw enter, laying down an irresistible rockish beat. Majestic solos follow from Harley, Rollins and Masuo, and after cogent interludes from bass and drums the horns return, taking the tune out with an euphoric gusto that had the crowd baying for more.

The Cutting Edge is not just full of top-notch improvising and mercurial inspiration. It is throughout characterised by a searing joyfulness – a quality that at times has been absent in Rollins's work. The album captures him in the highest of spirits, having an old-fashioned ball as well as working as hard as could be imagined. The point is an important one, because a joyous Rollins is a serene Rollins, and while not every artist produces his best work in the state of euphoric assurance, I am convinced that Sonny Rollins does do so.

Over a year would pass before Rollins's next Milestone album, but in November 1974 he played a concert in Belgrade which has recently become available on Jazz Door 1271. **First Moves** comprises four numbers played by a quintet featuring Masuo, Lee, bassist Gene Perla and Harley on soprano and bagpipes. The lengthy but always absorbing *Look For The Silver Lining* continues Rollins's life-long penchant for unusual material, and he and Harley explore it with cogency, wit and charm. There is another beautiful reading of *To A Wild Rose* – essentially a duet for tenor and guitar – and Harley's bagpipes add colour and bite to a rollicking version of *Alfie's Theme*. Recorded sound is only moderate at times, and Rollins's tone is often very different from his playing on **The Cutting Edge**, but it's a valuable addition to his discography.

The critical reputation of **Nucleus**, recorded in September 1975, is in the main modest and in several instances very low. Scott Yanow thinks it exemplifies the "disappointment" many Rollins followers feel at his 70s and 80s recordings and complains that it "falls far short of hinting at any new innovations (*sic*)."[48] Cook & Morton's *Penguin Guide* goes further, suggesting that it courts "outright disaster... the band have his feet chained, and none of the tracks takes off."[49] All those remarks could judiciously be applied to some of Rollins's later Milestone work, but as assessments of **Nucleus** they are both unjust and unconvincing. The album may not be amongst Rollins's very best, but it is full of imagination and idiomatic flair; *pace* Yanow there are new things a-plenty, and *pace* Cook & Morton the extrovert numbers have an unchained, hard-driving gutsiness.

Perhaps these critics and others were put off by the fusion ethos that attends much of the album's music; certainly, the four Rollins originals that make up the LP's first side and Mtume's *Newkleus* find him investigating fusion territory in his most thoroughgoing fashion yet. But nearly all of it works and indeed exhilarates, from the funky stomping of *Are You Ready* to the gritty soulfulness of *Lucille* (written for Mrs. Rollins). *Newkleus* is reminiscent of Herbie Hancock's almost exactly contemporaneous **Manchild** and **Secrets** (which I consider a strength), while *Cosmet* is another reminder of Rollins the prophet of hard bop: he solos with swinging authority, as do trombonist Raul de Souza[50] and Bennie Maupin on lyricon. Finally, *My Reverie* is a lovely excursion in its own right and also makes for an intriguing comparison with the reading on **Tenor Madness.**[51] All three horns shine, and pianist George Duke also impresses.

The personnel for **Nucleus** – ten musicians in all – was the largest ever featured on a Rollins album, apart from the four big band tracks for Verve under Leonard Feather's auspices. As one might expect from a Rollins date, however, the ten were deployed variously. Only Maupin and guitarist David Amaro play on all seven selections; Duke is absent on two tracks; Mtume doesn't get to play on his own *Newkleus*; the rhythm section alternates between Bob Cranshaw and Roy McCurdy (*Newkleus, My Reverie* and *Azalea*) and Chuck Rainey and Eddie Moore on the other four cuts. Such changes hint at restlessness, even eccentricity; nevertheless, whatever the configuration, on this occasion the band emerges as a formidably cohesive unit.

The phrase "on this occasion" is important. If I have a much higher opinion of **Nucleus** than many others do, I must grant that it signified a change in approach that did not serve Rollins's art as well as he must have hoped. As Dave Gelly observed in 1983 when reviewing **No Problem** (q.v.):

> This is band music, and Rollins has never really been a band player. The format seems to tie him down; the very organisation of the music prevents him from imposing his own organisation upon it. As a result, he sounds on some tunes like any good Hollywood session player. Of course he plays well, because he's incapable of playing badly, but there is none of the characteristic

> asperity, that rigorous pulling apart and re-ordering, which made Sonny Rollins the great artist he is ... I can't believe that a man of such legendary determination and self-knowledge looks upon this record as a serious addition to his life's work. [52]

Both tone and analysis are perfectly judged; all I would add is that **No Problem** was not so much a *newly* sad development as the latest in a series of albums charting a marked decline in creativity from those first four.

I will pass quickly over **The Way I Feel** (1976). The controlling idea may have seemed attractive – Rollins playing alongside session musicians and guest stars, and accompanied by such fusion luminaries as Lee Ritenour and Billy Cobham. But as Gelly observes, 'band music' has never been Rollins's *metier*, and here that problem is doubly compounded by mundane material and the decision to dub in the guest horn section. The results are, in Cook & Morton's words, "plain feeble": the music is airless and formulaic, emasuclating Rollins's matchless *extempore* strengths, and it cannot be accidental that the album is not represented on that 2-CD **Silver City** compilation.

Easy Living (1977) restores Rollins to a quintet setting, and some of it is excellent – the title track and the leader's soprano work on *My One And Only Love* and *Arroz Con Pollo* (where drummer Tony Williams is inspired). However, the album opens with two disco-music tracks, and they do not impress. I cannot share the outer sleeve's enthusiasm for *Isn't She Lovely*. In all truth Stevie Wonder's original (on **Songs In The Key Of Life**) is superior, and one suspects that Rollins's reasons for recording it were as much commercial as artistic. No harm in that, and one is pleased to learn that it nearly became a hit for him;[53] but while his reading is perfectly okay, one expects rather more than that from Rollins. *Down The Line* is pleasant in much the same inconsequential way, and although the ten-minute closer *Hear What I'm Saying* gives Rollins plenty of room to stretch out, the results are less riveting than one would like.

Don't Stop The Carnival preserves some of the music Rollins played over three days at the Great American Music Hall in San Francisco in April 1978. It is as uneven as its predecessor: *Autumn Nocturne* is exquisite and *Silver City* also impresses; but the rest of the programme is thin. Even the title track pales into nothingness when one recalls Rollins's many subsequent versions of the song (especially those in concert), and the presence on some tracks of a dreadfully out-of-sorts Donald Byrd doesn't help. The album further bears out the wisdom of Gelly's words above: the band music items fail to grip, and by far its best moments are when Rollins assumes full control.

The autumn of 1978 found Rollins in the company of McCoy Tyner, Ron Carter and Al Foster for **The Milestone Jazz All Stars In Concert**. The tracks are taken from four different dates and are commensurately various in format – solo performances by Rollins, Tyner and Carter; Tyner in tandem with Carter (a superb reading of *Alone Together*) and Rollins; *Don't Stop The Carnival* for pianoless trio; and three quartet performances, one of which (*Nubia*) features Rollins on soprano. The disparate mixture is thoroughly absorbing, and everyone plays very well; however, the most striking feature is Tyner's pianism. His work throughout is orchestral in grandeur, and on the opening *The Cutting Edge* Rollins seems temporarily outfaced, having presumably never heard that composition endowed with such sonorous weight before. But he recovers, and the rest of the album finds him relishing the pianist's genius. Especially fine are Carter's exuberant *N.O.Blues*, which inspires a thrilling Rollins solo, and the duet with Tyner, *In A Sentimental Mood*, which is creative partnership of the first order. It is moments such as these that prompted my Part Two reflections on what working with a pianist of Tyner's stature might have brought forth in Rollins's music, particularly when one remembers the magnificent work of a contemporaneous tenor-piano combination – Stan Getz and Kenny Barron.

Those last remarks will strike some as whimsical, but I doubt if many can turn from Rollins' work with the All Stars to his next four Milestone albums without falling prey to some degree of depression. **Don't Ask** is an almost astonishing curate's egg. The two duets with guitarist Larry Coryell (*The File* and *My Ideal*) are stirring; the title track has a most attractive melody; and *Tai-Chi* is certainly different – a plaintive orientalesque line played on the lyricon. The rest of the album is the acme of pallid vulgarity. *Harlem Boys* and *And Then My Love I Found You* are bad enough – neither decent jazz nor good dance music – but dubious pride of place must go to *Disco Monk*. What on earth was Rollins about here? To perpetrate – and release – this farrago was one thing; to brand it with the name of the man whose difficult music he understood better than practically anyone else and with whom he had done work of high distinction was quite another. Crass and lumpish, it is without doubt the worst thing he has ever recorded.

If one is spared such unique ghastliness on Rollins's next three albums, there is little of distinction either. There are occasional pleasures: *The Very Thought of You* and *Double Feature* (a duet with Stanley Clarke) on **Love At First Sight**; a lovely reading of Billy Strayhorn's *My Little Brown Book* on **Reel Life**; the title track from **No Problem.** But in the main the music is lacklustre; Scott Yanow has noticed that "he often coasts on his own originals"[54] – a damaging tendency, as such material had for some time dominated his studio work – and the inference is that Rollins was becoming tired. That might explain the otherwise mystifying decision on **Love At First Sight** to revisit *Strode Rode*. Al Foster plays well, especially in the exchange of fours with Rollins, and George Duke noodles away conscientiously; however, the performance is nothing to write home about even in its own right, and to anyone conversant with the majestic version on **Saxophone Colossus** it is not just embarrassing but sad.

If Rollins was in need of a rest, it is not I hope unkind to detect a similar lassitude on Milestone's part, in the shape of perfunctory annotation and uninspired art work. There appear to have been no 'artist-*versus*-executives' tensions: Rollins's relationship with the company has always been (and remains) harmonious. But with the notable exception of the **Milestone All Stars Concert** – and that was a maverick – the heady achievements of **Next Album** and **The Cutting Edge** must have seemed a distant memory, and it would have taken a brave person to predict that his next visit to the studio would produce the best album Rollins had cut in ten years.

Before turning to **Sunny Days, Starry Nights**, however, I want to consider in some detail assessments of Rollins's Milestone work offered by Gary Giddins over a twenty-year period. As good a writer on jazz as the music has seen, Giddins has always been a perceptive champion of Rollins's work, drawing this tribute from the tenorist himself:

> Gary Giddins cares about jazz. He also cares about the people who spend their lives trying to create it. You may not always agree with him, but his opinions always make for provocative, interesting, and valuable reading.[55]

It is therefore appropriate that he was entrusted with what amounts to the Foreword to the **Silver City** compilation, which begins:

> How's this for a critic's wet dream? Impatient at the flippant, glib, and ignorant dismissal of a quarter of a century of Sonny Rollins's finest work, you write an article suggesting his label compile a selection of milestone (to coin a phrase) performances, listing what you believe those performances to be. Then you learn that the label was intending to do just that, and furthermore that Sonny and Lucille found themselves in agreement with your list and augmented it to fill out the space of two discs. Then the label sends you a generous and entirely unexpected check, because they feel that in effect you have co-edited the anthology ...[56]

Giddins is right to be pleased with the anthology: give or take the inevitable quibble fans will have about this inclusion or that omission, it is both representative and satisfying. But two things should be said. First, it is unjust to brand all criticism of Rollins's Milestone output as "flippant, glib and ignorant". I can think of few less apposite descriptions of critics Dave Gelly, Michael Shera, Chris Sheridan or Keith Shadwick, all of whom have written with erudite incisiveness on the work concerned. Nor is the noun "dismissal" justified. To find something inferior or less than fully satisfying does not imply outright rejection, and the tone of those writers – and others such as Cook & Morton and Scott Yanow – is invariably one of judicious sadness rather than dismissive.

Second, Giddins's 'There's No One Like Sonny Rollins', an account of the tenorist's work written across 1976-80, scarcely amounts to a paean of praise.[57] He has nothing like as high an opinion as I do of **The Cutting Edge**, which he finds compromised both by Harley – "one in a string of flashy guest stars" – and by "undistinguished material" further undermined by "a cluttered rhythm section". **Nucleus** he thinks "more intriguing" but deleteriously chequered; **The Way I Feel** was "a desperate attempt to enter the soulsax sweepstakes"; **Don't Stop The Carnival** is judged "graphically disappointing (in that) the highs and lows are so extreme." And if he is kinder to **Don't Ask** than I can be, the observation that it has "episodes to recommend it but little more" is itself close to a dismissal.

My observations are not an attempt to score cheap points at the expense of a distinguished critic. Far from it: local disagreements notwithstanding, I think Giddins is right. He regularly refers back to Rollins's 50s work in a predominantly wistful fashion with which I identify wholeheartedly. In doing so he is no more "flippant" or "ignorant" than others who have found the majority of Rollins's Milestone output inferior to his definitive work, but it has to be said that such trenchancy does not sit easily alongside his 1996 impatience at the "dismissal of a quarter of a century of Sonny Rollins's finest work." To be fair, however, the latter remark *is* more in tune with the tone and judgments of his 1984 'Euphoria',[58] extracts from which form the epigraph to this chapter.

The essay centres on a celebration of **Sunny Days, Starry Nights**, which Giddins regards as a major breakthrough for Rollins:

> For several years he's been moving in the direction of a music that suggests the fires of blessed inspiration with none of the penalties. His intonation has grown, quite literally: it's fatter, grittier, more colorful, and less sour than ever before... The most rhythmically inventive musician of his generation, he seems to have realized that the Ur-calypso he's been exploring for nearly 30 years has become his mandate, a key to his current vision. The result is a fervent positivism that, far from being easily won – think of all the misfires of the past decade – celebrates its victory over the night in every measure...
>
> Rollins was never comfortable with the lavish disclosures of self, the musical glossolalia, the narcissim let loose in the wake of Coltrane. He had to make his own way through the excesses of freedom, fusion, and tradition, and with this new album he seems finally to have resolved a host of ambivalences.[59]

The eloquence of the second paragraph is complemented by Giddins's masterly analysis of the album's music. The opening *Mava Mava* is indeed "superb Rollins", and "euphoric . . unabashed dance music" perfectly describes *Tell Me You Love Me*, which is a striking contrast to the tenorist's earlier (rather dismal) genuflections in the direction of Grover Washington. Giddins is also suitably impressed by the reading of Noel Coward's *I'll See You Again* and the vigorous but affectionate deconstruction of *I'm Old Fashioned*. I am even more taken than he is with *Wynton*:[60] the tempo is courageously languid, and although Giddins is persuasive in observing that "only the leader seems to know exactly where he's going", the results are nonetheless as cohesive as graceful.

Sunny Days, Starry Nights is additionally important in marking the recorded debut as Rollins sidemen of trombonist

Clifton Anderson and pianist Mark Soskin: they would form the nucleus of his regular group for a number of years to come. Though not remotely in the tenorist's league as a soloist, Anderson proved a useful foil from the start, adding colour and texture to the ensemble, while Soskin demonstrates an intuitive understanding of his boss's needs as well as soloing with taste and charm. In all, the album is as warming as successful, heralding a newly settled Rollins who was ready both to consolidate serenely and seek out further challenges.

His next record certainly belongs in that latter category. **The Solo Album** was cut in July 1985; comprising two performances of nearly half an hour each, it could be seen as the pinnacle of Rollins's commitment to the art of improvisation. Not everyone saw it that way: Scott Yanow pronounces it "one of the few complete duds of [his] career,"[61] and Cook & Morton express major reservations:

> Solo Rollins isn't necessarily the same thing as a Rollins solo ... This anchorless solo concert too often relies on scales and practice patterns, as if he were woodshedding for the real thing. It's an opportunity to hear and study his grainy, utterly distinctive tone at length, but note for note this scarcely stands with solo sax albums which the avant-garde masters have produced.[62]

I am not persuaded by that last remark: Rollins's efforts compare well to those of Anthony Braxton and David Murray. But Cook & Morton's overall case is cogent: the album is very hard work, and it does not always seem worth it. Light, shade and dynamics tend to be sacrificed, and though I cannot agree with Yanow that the album amounts to "56 minutes of wandering around", it is not one I play very often, preferring the much shorter and wholly absorbing *Continuum* on the **Milestone Jazz All Stars In Concert**.

The Solo Album was recorded in the Sculpture Garden of NYC's Museum of Modern Art. So, a year later, was **G-Man**, which was made available both as a film and on record.[63] The title track is vintage Rollins. He looks in superb physical shape, with the coiled energy of a man half his age, and the music just pours out of him, densely structured for all its carefree spontaneity and with impeccable dynamic range. The session also features an attractive Rollins line, *Kim*, and a superior version of *Don't Stop The Carnival*. In audio terms, things then get a little complicated. The CD configuration adds a fourth NYC performance, the twelve-minute *Tenor Madness*; the LP includes instead a work recorded in Japan, *Concerto For Tenor Saxophone And Symphony Orchestra*, and it is that I now want to address.

Sadly, the *Concerto* is a muted work. Rollins plays beautifully, and his themes are wonderfully strong; however, Heikki Sarmanto's orchestration is not in the same class. It is a pity that Rollins did not think to collaborate with Toru Takemitsu, the distinguished Japanese composer with a strong interest in jazz, who might have mobilised Rollins's fascination with both space and Japanese culture in a truly memorable way. That said, I do not find the Sarmanto session as much of an embarrassment as do some Rollins devotees of my acquaintance: Rollins's playing is too good for that, and there are some felicitous moments from the orchestra. It's just that the arrangements, superficially clever, lack the tenorist's penetration, so that his themes are domesticated rather than fully harnessed. The closest parallel that occurs to me is Stan Getz's **Communications 72**, where equally majestic tenor playing is similarly compromised by facile writing.[64]

At the time of writing Rollins has made six further Milestone albums; all of them reflect the restored focus and renewed promise signalled by **Sunny Days, Starry Nights** without ever quite reaching the highest peaks. **Dancing In The Dark** has a deliciously stringent *I'll String Along With You*, several sturdy Rollins originals and a very fine reading of the title track. **Falling In Love With Jazz** varies in personnel. *For All We Know* and *I Should Care* reunite Rollins with Tommy Flanagan and with predictably excellent results: these cuts also add the tenor sax of

Branford Marsalis, whose presence clearly invigorates the leader. Three tracks, including a splendid *Falling In Love with Love,* have on hand regulars Anderson, Soskin and Cranshaw, with guitarist Jerome Harris and Jack DeJohnette completing the sextet. Anderson is absent from *Little Girl Blue* and *Tennessee Waltz,* which is to my mind the most contentious performance on the whole album.

The problem is not the tune itself – by now, any Rollins enthusiast was both used to such recondite choices and revelled in them – or the tenorist's own playing, but the arrangement and musical ethos, which leans heavily in the direction of Country & Western. Fair enough, it might be argued; after all, the tune is a C & W classic. But ultimately it is not very edifying to listen to Rollins trying to wail over a background designed for Tammy Wynette. *Tennessee Waltz* appears on **Silver City**: that, too, is fair enough, since the track is undoubtedly striking in its own fashion. But I have to part company with that compilation's chief annotator, Chip Stern, when he writes:

> There's nothing so undervalued as the collected works of Sonny Rollins from 1972 through 1996... Tell me, why does our tolerance for ditties like *Wagon Wheels* not extend to *Isn't She Lovely* or *Tennessee Waltz*?[65]

The answer is simple: *Wagon Wheels* is immeasurably *better*, if the criterion is Rollins's use of the material – and what other can there be? In addition, on that classic Rollins had inspired support from Ray Brown and Shelly Manne at their imaginative best; on *Tennessee Waltz* – through no fault of their own – Mark Soskin and Jack DeJohnette sound not only uncomfortable but positively clumsy.

Here's To The People is cheerily communicative if somewhat routine for the most part. However, *I Wish I knew* and *Young Roy* add the outstanding young trumpeter Roy Hargrove, and while it would be overstating the case to say that this partnership takes us back forty years to Clifford Brown, the presence of a class act up front makes a significant difference both to Rollins's playing and the music overall.

As I approach the end of this chapter and move towards a consideration of Rollins's overall achievement, it is pleasing to report that his three most recent albums are of high quality. **Old Flames** is a distinguished collection of ballad readings enhanced by Jimmy Heath's deft arrangements for the accompanying brass choir. Cook & Morton draw proper attention to the tenorist's "magisterial voice", but I do not find the record as "sombre" as they do:[66] the successful work of a great artist is always uplifting even when the accent is on tragedy, which characterises *I See Your Face Before Me* in particular.

Sonny Rollins + 3, is a deeply satisfying set of performances: the redoubtable Cranshaw is present throughout, joined either by Tommy Flanagan with Al Foster or young lion Stephen Scott with DeJohnette. Both groups shine fiercely; all material comes alike to them, be it Rollins originals *Biji* and *H.S.* or such standards as *What A Difference A Day Made* and *Mona Lisa,* and Rollins is in the kind of imperious form that recalls the old days; the final track, twelve minutes of *I've Never Been In Love Before*, is especially commanding.

Finally, **Global Warming**, made at two seperate sessions in January and February 1998, dramatises anew the political dimension of Rollins's work. The hue this time is not black but green – the fate of planet Earth. On the sleeve Rollins concludes his brief poem on the subject with the observation "Not that much time left neither," and the title track, *Mother Nature's Blues* and *Clear-Cut Boogie* ("clear-cutting" is a euphemism for destroying whole tracts of forest) enshrine this ecological concern in stirringly unpretentious fashion. The alarmist titular implications of *Global Warming* do not prevent the music taking off in fiercely joyous vein, rendering the track an inspirational call to arms rather than a doomwatch lament, while *Clear-Cut Boogie* has a memorable line and some darkly sonorous harmonies that contrive to be both menacing and exhilirating at once. Elsewhere there's a fine reading of Irving Berlin's *Change Partners* and Rollins's quite delightful *Island Lady*, and in all the album impresses as one of Rollins's strongest Milestones. It is a heartening note on which to end this section of my account.

Notes

1 Giddins, *Rhythm-a-ning*, 268.

2 2257 readers voted for Coltrane; runner-up Stan Getz – smack in the middle of his lucrative and musically resplendent bossa nova period – polled 1547. Rollins was third with just 423, while the rapidly emerging Archie Shepp came in at six, with 124 votes.

3 It still does – and the number of acolytes has clearly grown. Coltrane remains as influential now as he was then, as the work of *inter alia* Michael Brecker, Ralph Moore, Joe Henderson and Jan Garbarek testifies.

4 *All What Jazz*, 65.

5 *Ibid*, 172 and 166. The records in question are, respectively, **Meditation** and **Ascension** (both on Impulse!).

6 For those interested in such a discussion, it will be found in my forthcoming *Philip Larkin: "Deceptions": Creating Harmony Out Of Discord* (Hull University Press: probably Spring 1999).

7 *All What Jazz*, 19.

8 Kingsley Amis, 'A New James Bond', *What Became of Jane Austen?* (London: Panther, 1972), 68.

9 On a comparative note: I have been a reviewer for *Jazz Journal International* since 1978, in which twenty years I have written some 850 record reviews (slightly fewer than Larkin in twice the time) and about fifty book reviews (slightly more).

10 Joseph Epstein, 'Mr. Larkin Gets A Life', *Life Sentences* (Norton: 1997), 241.

11 *All What Jazz*, 18-19.

12 For example: "(Fats) Navarro was a good, a very good bop trumpeter, better if you like than the young Miles Davis, and even pushing Clifford Brown. But what does that mean? Only that he was able to play fast, high, screwy trumpet better than they could." (*All What Jazz*, 236). Tetchy and disagreeable though that is, the point requires an answer, even if it's not very difficult to come up with one.

13 *All What Jazz*, 29.

14 Written for his monthly *Daily Telegraph* column, the piece was never published. Larkin fell foul of what now can be seen as a precursor of Political Correctness: I have little doubt that his tough, though not entirely unsympathetic, words were deemed to be not in tune with the prevailing Coltrane hagiography, so out

they went. (They are fully restored in *All What Jazz*, 186-8.)

Larkin got some sort of revenge three years later, when in one of his last columns he marked the death of altoist Johnny Hodges with the sentence: "Hodges brought as much beauty into jazz as Coltrane did ugliness (a large claim but I'll stick to it), but Coltrane got *The Times* obituary and Hodges didn't: that's the world we live in." (*All What Jazz*, 257).

15 Michael Jackson, *Sonny Rollins: The Search For Self Through Art* (Unpublished dissertation, University of Brighton, 1988), 44. Mr Jackson's survey is full of insight, and it deserves a much wider currency than it can currently enjoy. A personal anecdote might serve to illustrate just how dramatic was the slump he identifies.

In 1966 I went up to Cambridge (to read English) and was delighted to find a thriving University Jazz Club. Sessions at the Red Lion pub in Pety Cury attracted audiences of up to a hundred week in, week out. The musicians were mainly local amateurs or undergraduates (including at least two who went on to have professional careers in jazz – Steve Cook and Daryl Runswick) but there were also regular appearances by professionals. In my first term I remember seeing Bobby Wellins, Danny Moss and Harry Becket, all of whom charged about a fiver plus expenses. In addition, special concerts could command large venues with audiences to match: Ben Webster and Teddy Wilson were two such attractions.

When I graduated three years later, the Club was about to fold. It had lost a fair amount of money on the Teddy Wilson concert, but that would not have been a problem had those weekly Red Lion sessions still been thriving. They were not: only a few die-hards continued to attend, and funds no longer ran to inviting visits from professionals even at the picayune rates just mentioned. The Beatles, ersatz folk music and rock in general had taken over – an anglicised echo of the way American blacks in their droves had turned from jazz to soul. Jazz, so it suddenly seemed, was unmarketable in the town. With a matter of months three record shops that had regularly supplied my needs virtually stopped stocking jazz altogether, and so began my long dependence on the London specialist shops. And as a kind of grimly appropriate postscript: the 1970s saw the demolition of the Red Lion, along with all of Pety Cury, to make way for a shopping precinct that to this day retains all the soulful charm of a discarded hamburger container.

16 Jackson, 44.

17 *New York Times*, June 7, 1993.

18 Patterson, *Grand Expectations*, 373.

19 *Ibid*, 373.

20 *Ibid*, 373.

21 It was inevitable that as rock mushroomed in popularity and 'social significance' individual tragedies would follow. The deaths of Jimi Hendrix and ex-Rolling Stone Brian Jones were two such; the case of Brian Epstein is arguably even more affecting.

In some respects his success was an example of Duke Ellington's celebrated formula – "Being at the right place at the right time with the right thing before the right people". But if that is a definition of luck, it is also (as Ellington himself was aware) a definition of genius. Somehow Epstein just knew that the raw energy of the Beatles – and also that of minor, now-forgotten acts like Tommy Quickly, Peter & Gordon and The Foremost – could be harnessed into something the young would go without food to hear and buy. Though he had little liking for pop music as such, Epstein knew a goldmine when he heard it; he also had that "infinite capacity for taking pains" that many associate with genius. His meticulous packaging of the Beatles alone proves that: the innovative suits, the hair-cuts, the cannily showcased Scouse accents, the no less carefully orchestrated wacky humour – all these (and more) Beatle-traits testified to Epstein's Midas touch as a commodity broker.

But his genius did not extend to the minutiae of marketing or indeed to the world of big money, into which the colossal success of 'The Liverpool Sound' soon pitched him; he was also a vulnerable and unhappy human being. Both weaknesses are pithily summarised in *The Penguin Encyclopedia of Popular Music*:

> [Epstein's] worst mistake was letting USA rights to Beatle merchandise go for almost nothing. Homosexual with unhappy love life, reportedly in love with John Lennon; losing control of the Beatles (whose contract soon to expire); heavily into drugs, especially sleeping pills; died suddenly, probably of accidental cumulative overdose, though suicide mooted and enemies had threatened violence. Death shocked Beatles; Lennon said they would never made it without him.

Lennon was surely right, and his remark confirms the Frankensteinian tragedy that was Brian Epstein. He was consumed by the monster he had created – in stark contrast to Colonel Tom Parker's monster, which (almost literally) consumed only itself.

22 Everyone's except mine, that is. In a way, I shall always be grateful to them: my 'conversion' to jazz in 1964 at the age of seventeen was the result of a desperate bid to find something to listen to other than the Beatles, who monopolised every gathering or programme on hand and whom I alone in the Western world, it seemed, couldn't stick at any price. But their colossal appeal has always baffled me. It was hard enough to credit when it was all hysterically going on, but quite why their facile charm continues to enchant in a wholly different time and concourse of circumstances is even more mystifying. Maybe the explanation is nostalgia, led by parents who were the 60s young; or maybe it's just that current pop is even less satisfying.

23 *Louisville Times*, 9 December, 1967.

24 Don Demichael, 'A Long Look At Stan Getz', *Down Beat*, xxxiii / 5 (1966), 19. The essay contains a story which Getz delighted in recounting, concerning an incident on a JATP tour: 'We were all tired, and everbody was sort of asleep on the bus. Pres was sitting in an aisle seat, dozing, when a well-known saxophonist took out his ax and began walking up and down the aisle playing licks. Nobody paid any attention to him, so finally he went over to Lester and said, "Hey, Pres, whaddya think of that?" Pres, his eyes half-closed, said, "Yes, Lady (expletive deleted), but can you sing me a song?".' Various suggestions have been put forward about the identity of the 'offending' tenor player: the consensus seems to favour Sonny Stitt.

25 Ian Carr, *Miles Davis* (London: Paladin, 1984), 196.

26 The album was **What The World Needs Now**, recorded in August 1967 (Verve LP V6-8725).

27 Carr, 203.

28 *Ibid*, 221.

29 As witness the electrifying *Woody's Boogaloo* on **Concerto For Herd** (Verve SVLP 9235; not available on CD) and certain tracks on his 1968 album **Light My Fire** (Cadet CRLS 4544; ditto).

30 Davis's **In A Silent Way** and **ESP** are on Columbia CS 9875 and CL 2350 respectively. Hancock's **Headhunters** is on Columbia Sony CK 65123; Herman's **Heavy Exposure** is on Cadet 6467 308 (LP only) and **Giant Steps** on Fantasy FCD 609 9432; Getz's **Captain Marvel** is on Columbia Sony COL 468412 2.

As noted in the main text, the majority of 70s fusion jazz has in my view failed to match those records' success in standing the test of time. It is clear, however, that plenty of people do not agree – including (it is safe to assume) the Board and senior executives at Columbia Sony. In the last two years the company has reissued Weather Report's *oeuvre* and Hancock's funk output in their entirety and its Legacy programme has made newly available work by Tom Scott, George Duke and Tony Williams. Moreover, it has acquired the rights to CTI, the label Creed Taylor founded on leaving Verve, and in 1997 its 'CTI Catalogue Re-Launch Series' reissued a dozen albums with the promise of more to come. If some items – by Lalo Schifrin, Hubert Laws, Milt Jackson – are more than welcome, it's impossible to be similarly enthusiastic about resuscitated Deodato or Patti Austin.

Although it would be churlish to deride such marketing enterprise, the revival of interest it evidences is odd in the extreme. The music is for the most part decidedly jejeune and I wonder what the musicians themselves make of it all. In a recent review of Tony Williams's 1970 album (**Turn It Over**) Mark Gilbert shrewdly remarks, "He moved further away from convention, towards a rather grotesque form of progressive rock ... before returning, *like, it seems, everybody else*, to proper jazz in the eighties." (*Jazz Journal International*, li / 4 (1998); my emphasis.) Gilbert has observed to me since that his "proper jazz" is ironic in intention; that granted, his point is still in harmony with my argument. Fusion may have been the shot in the arm a debilitated jazz needed in the dying days of the 60s, but it was a passing phase, and I would guess that the new lease of life it has been granted is a cause of embarrassment to many, musicians and listeners alike – akin to catching sight of old photographs where one is sporting flares and vastly unpleasant kipper ties.

31 In 1971 Granz had said to Leonard Feather, "It's an outrage that of the twenty seven albums I produced with Art Tatum not a single one is available – they've all been deleted from the catalog ... I even tried to buy the masters back, just so I could get them on the market again, but they wouldn't let me have them." Early in Granz's Pablo days, Verve relented: he re-issued them all during 1975. They are now available as single CDs and in two box set collections, **The Tatum Solo Masterpieces** (Pablo 7PACD 4404-2) and the **Tatum Group Masterpieces** (Pablo 2405 424/431-2).

Granz's Pablo initiative deserves an extensive gloss, for it turned out to be hardly less momentous and valuable than his earlier achievements. The label's launch was deceptively conservative, its first four issues appearing to signal a return to the ethos of Verve and JATP. The 3-LP **Jazz At The Santa Monica** Civic offered sets by the Basie Orchestra, on its own and with Ella Fitzgerald; a JATP-style package featuring Getz, 'Lockjaw' Davis, Eldridge and Harry Edison; and a recreation of Oscar Peterson's1949 American debut with Ray Brown. Of the three accompanying single LP issues, one featured Peterson and another Fitzgerald; since Granz was personal manager to both artists, some critics were ready to curl the lip at a predictably cosy set-up. But the third nipped such a reaction in the bud: **Duke Ellington's Big Four**, with Brown, Joe Pass and Mickey Roker, was rightly hailed as an innovative and inspired date.

And that album epitomised the real ethos of Pablo. Granz rescued the careers of Sarah Vaughan and Roy Eldridge: both had gone over five years without recording, and both now produced some of their finest-ever work in his studios. The music of Dizzy Gillespie – for some time in the doldrums – underwent a stunning renascence via such albums as **Bahiana, Dizzy Gillespie's Big Four, Afro-Cuban Jazz Moods** and (perhaps above all) his duo with Peterson. When the Modern Jazz Quartet disbanded in 1974 (it would re-form some years later) Granz signed Milt Jackson and at once presided over a series of recordings that must be judged amongst the vibist's very best – particularly his work at the 1975 Montreux Jazz Festival, which Granz recorded in its entirety. (He did the same two years later – an even larger-scale event than its predecessor.)

Other musicians who were major beneficiaries of his vision included Benny Carter, pianists Ray Bryant and Tommy Flanagan, Zoot Sims, Clark Terry and blues singer Joe Turner. Pablo also made a major star of guitarist Joe Pass, rejuvenated the Basie Orchestra and in putting together Jackson, Brown, Pass and Roker created one of the finest latter-day chamber groups, Quadrant. And while Fitzgerald's voice was no longer the divine instrument it had been in those Verve days, Granz served her music with distinction, placing her in sympathetic contexts that showed off her still-infallible musicianship to the full.

Finally, Peterson's Pablo *oeuvre* is a monument to Granz's imagination and daring. As with Fitzgerald, Granz made no attempt to revisit past triumphs, going out of his way to present the pianist with fresh challenges – playing the clavichord on a new reading of **Porgy And Bess** with Joe Pass; 'jousts' with five separate trumpeters (Gillespie, Eldridge, Terry, Edison and Jon Faddis); dates with Jackson and with harmonica player Toots

Thielemans; the 'Satch & Josh' sessions with Basie. And he also ensured that Peterson's new career as a solo concert artist was properly documented: the set on **A Salle Pleyel** remains the pianist's greatest on record.

Why such a long note about an impresario who had nothing to do with Rollins's work of the time? Well, the label was decisively instrumental in re-establishing a market and an enthusiasm for mainstream jazz, including a renewed interest in jazz recorded a generation before. By the time Granz sold Pablo to Fantasy in 1987, such solid recuperation was fast becoming a major renascence thanks to the advent of the CD. Jazz was commercially viable again, to an extent that would have been unimaginable fifteen years previously.

32 Kopulos, *op cit*, 30.

33 On Magnetic Records MRCD 118.

34 On Moon MCD 037-2 & 038-2.

35 Gitler, *Down Beat* xxxvi / 11 (1969), 19.

36 Bob Porter, 'This Man Called Sonny Rollins', *Down Beat*, xli / 3 (1974), 16.

37 *Ibid*, 16.

38 See Note 35.

39 *Ibid*, 18.

40 *Ibid*, 18.

41 From the booklet accompanying **Sonny Rollins Alternatives**, RCA ND 90651.

42 From the booklet accompanying **Silver City** (Milestone 2MCD 2501), 5.

43 *Ibid*, 5.

44 See Part One, page 19.

45 N.B. *Love Man* is not a typo: like *Notes for Eddie* it is a Rollins original, and should not be confused (as has been done) with *Lover Man*, the wonderful song written by Jimmy Davis, Roger 'Ram' Ramirez and Jimmy Sherman.

46 Herman's set included a tribute to Duke Ellington, *Tantum Ergo*; a blistering version of Billy Cobham's *Crosswind*; and similarly intelligent, fusion-infused readings of *Superstar* and *I Can't Get Next To You*. [The latter, originally a hit for The Temptations, had been a highlight of **Heavy Exposure**, featuring a marvellous solo by Herman stalwart Sal Nistico.] However, the *pièce de*

resistance was tenorist Gary Anderson's magnificent arrangement of Aaron Copland's *Fanfare For The Common Man*, one of the the finest things ever laid down by Herman's latterday bands. The concert was issued as **Herd At Montreux** (Fantasy LP F-9470) and, not before time was issued on CD in September 1998 (OJCCD 991-2).

47 Rollins's investigation of the tenor saxophone's drone effects owes something to Coltrane and his own aforementioned interest in Eastern music and philosophy. Tenor-drone can be said to approximate the '*OM*' incantation central to Eastern spiritual practice, and which Coltrane made the title of one of his records. Part of this performance's riveting power and musical originality lies in its amalgam of the Afro-American spiritual and its analogously fundamental Eastern equivalent, and it is a matter for considerable regret that Rollins did not explore this exciting new territory further.

48 *All Music Guide To Jazz*, 629.

49 *Penguin Guide To Jazz On CD, LP & Cassette*, 1113.

50 While De Souza did not record with Rollins again, the inference is that his trenchant contributions pleased the tenorist: a few years later he engaged another trombonist, Clifton Anderson, as his regular front-line partner.

51 See above, pages 35, and Note 34, Part One.

52 *Jazz Journal International*, xxxv / i (1983), 34-5.

53 See Gary Giddins, *Riding On A Blue Note: Jazz & American Pop* (New York: OUP, 1983), 124.

54 *All Music Guide To Jazz*, 629.

55 Quoted on the back blurb to *Riding On A Blue Note*.

56 **Silver City** booklet, 9.

57 *Riding On A Blue Note*, 120-30.

58 Collected in *Rhythm-a-ning*; see Part Two, Note 58.

59 *Ibid*, 268-9.

60 Neither the sleeve nor Giddins vouchsafes any notion of who might be the song's dedicatee; I wonder if it might be pianist Wynton Kelly, who had died in 1971. Giddins notes that the song shares a five-note phrase with Henry Mancini's *Charade*, but the line's subtle strength and melodic grace remind me strongly of the man who illuminated several Rollins albums of the 50s.

61 *All Music Guide To Jazz*, 629.

62 Cook & Morton, 1113.

63 The film was made by Robert Mugge and entitled *Saxophone Colossus*; in the UK the film was shown on Channel 4's series *Sounds Of Surprise*.

64 On Verve V6 8807 (LP only). Compositions and arrangements are by Michel Legrand.

65 **Silver City** booklet, 13.

66 Cook & Morton, 1114.

© Peter Symes

CONCLUSION: Rollins as saxophone colossus

> *Whenever I try to create anything when I'm playing solos, I try to blot out my mind as much as possible. Of course, I've already learned the material; then I try and blot out my mind and just let it flow by itself. So I try not not to think too much about what I'm playing: I have the structure already, and then I just try to let it come by itself.*
>
> Sonny Rollins, 1986

Rollins made those remarks during the film which produced *G-Man* and *Concerto For Tenor Saxophone and Symphony Orchestra*, and in several primary respects they go to the heart not only of his own playing but that of jazz itself. The combination of structural planning with almost muse-like inspiration is as good a working definition of jazz as any, and it is appropriate that the *oeuvre* of one of its greatest improvisers should dramatise that mélange so distinctively. And it is not the only conflation fundamental to jazz which his work illuminates.

Although still disputed in some quarters, it is an undoubted fact that "Jazz was always a hybrid, always an inspired accident."[1] Those words appear at the end of a recent essay by Alan Munton, and in exploring their implications in detail I want first to quote further from it. In the course of a compelling analysis of John Coltrane's *My Favourite Things* Munton pours scorn on the contention[2] that the piece is a riff, correctly identifying it as a rondo. He also observes that Coltrane "always plays three solos in each chorus of this piece" and continues:

> There is a musical reason for this: an alternation and contrast between major key and modal improvisations. Coltrane's first

> solo is a modal improvisation, whilst the second is in E major. Modal improvisation takes place upon a scale, in this case the Ionian scale on E ... Each formal device – the rondo, the chord sequence, the major key and the mode – is part of European musical practice. Coltrane's achievement is to have united European forms with rhythmic and improvisatory devices which originated in Africa.[3]

Selective quotation is always a delicate business, and I would not want anyone to infer from that last sentence a belief on Munton's part that this "achievement" was new. As he quickly points out in his next paragraph, every jazz musician in history has been

> ... obliged to work with European forms such as bar lines, diatonic chords, chord sequences and four-bar units of melody. They had already entered the blues form, which preceded jazz. They were taken over from a multitude of musical forms, such as the march, folk-song, and popular song, which arrived in North America from Europe during the nineteenth century. [4]

In short, jazz had been a Euro-African marriage from the outset and by definition. The one innovative feature which Munton claims for Coltrane's readings of Richard Rodgers's song – and then only implicitly – is their "level of emotional, rhythmic and melodic complexity";[5] to say that I can't go even that far is I hope more than a quibble. While I thrill to *My Favourite Things* as much as I assume Munton does, not only I can think of a number of contemporaneous records that are its equal in emotional intensity and musical complexity but more than a few earlier ones too. Indeed, the *locus classicus* has to be what is reputedly the only jazz performance never to be out of the catalogue – Louis Armstrong's *West End Blues*, recorded on June 28, 1928.

In contrast to Coltrane's marathons, *West End Blues* lasts three minutes and fifteen seconds, but it has *everything*. That epic opening cadenza that uses all twelve notes of the chromatic scale; solos of mellowness and depth from trombonist Fred Robinson and Jimmy Strong on clarinet; Earl Hines's astonishing interlude which to this day sounds years ahead of its time; a formal insight that simultaneously honours the blues form and takes it to a new level; and to crown all a solo from Armstrong that in the words of John Chilton is

> ... one of the most stirring and perfectly conceived choruses ever recorded. The final touch is sublime: a cascade of descending phrases from Louis gives way to a swirl of ingenious keyboard voicings, then Louis re-establishes the reflective opening mood, allowing his front-line partners to harmonize exquisitely with this concluding phrases. [6]

Total command is allied to an infallible sense of form in what Chilton calls "a triumphantly rounded performance": jazz does not come any better, more audacious or more masterly than this.

Its sustained and repeated brilliance notwithstanding, then, too much can be made of Coltrane's *My Favourite Things*. And if that last clause seems familiar, that is my intention: it echoes James Lincoln Collier's judgment of Rollins's *Blue Seven*, quoted in Part One.[7] He too cited an Armstrong performance (*Muggles*) in suggesting that the tenorist's approach was "hardly an innovation". One does not have to share Collier's view that "by 1960 the aging players of the dixieland school were producing more interesting music than the hard boppers"[8] to be suitably aware that a great deal of post-1940 jazz was a matter of refinement rather than fundamental innovation. As I observed early on, even the most spectacular 'changes' that bop effected were at most the full realisation of what had been implicit in the music of Duke Ellington and Art Tatum, and *West End Blues* shows the seeds were planted even earlier.

I think it is especially important to remember all this when addressing the work of Rollins, who throughout his career has been a modernist icon. While there is much in his work to justify that view, many of his most enduring strengths are essentially conservative. Like all distinguished Romantics, his art is a synthesis of the traditional and the radical – a property enshrined in his response to the three men who shaped his style.

Rollins got his conception of sound from Coleman Hawkins, of rhythm from Lester Young and of harmony from Charlie Parker. The summary is crude, but it will serve, not least because all three of his 'masters' similarly married the old and the new. Hawkins was necessarily a pioneer: nobody took the tenor saxophone seriously until he came along. But he also reflected the values of Armstrong and Beiderbecke; in addition, he was an erudite musician, as well-versed in the classical repertoire as in jazz. It was this quality as much as his admirable open-mindedness that explains his enthusiasm for Bebop. He knew that beneath the iconoclasm of the 'new' music lay an awareness of the momentous achievements of Debussy, Stravinsky, Bartok and Schoenberg, and that in terms of formal and harmonic sophistication jazz was catching up rather than ploughing new ground. It was a lesson Rollins took on board from the start.

Lester Young was no less literate; the apparently revolutionary nature of his sonic and rhythmic conception was firmly rooted in jazz's history. It is often forgotten that Young was a magnificent practitioner on jazz's 'senior' woodwind, the clarinet; indeed, he was reputedly the equal of Goodman or Artie Shaw. But that aspect of his genius was surplus to the requirements of the Basie orchestra and thus was hardly ever featured; nevertheless, his fondness for the instrument and for the rather 'feminine' C-melody saxophone made famous by Frankie Trumbauer help place in proper perspective the extraordinary impact of his debut recordings on tenor in 1936. In addition, his feeling for form and line were as profound as Armstrong's.[9]

So was Charlie Parker's. Armstrong was the first – and probably still the greatest – jazz artist to combine infallible structural insight with intuitively apposite spontaneity, but Parker's genius was just as comprehensive. The rhythmic acumen that accelerated the flowering of Bebop was his most obviously formidable quality, but he had a lightning appreciation of harmony and a mastery of form the equal of Hawkins, Young and Ellington. Like *West End Blues*, in fact, he had everything.

Or did he? These observations by Martin Williams are as cogent as they are provocative or even heretical:

> Parker's was a brilliant creative talent – perhaps a genius – but the more one goes over the work he left, the more incomplete it may appear ... How many of Parker's records have thew emotional form of finality of statement, of 'passion spent' at their end? Some. Probably not a majority ... Perhaps Parker was a musical genius who became a musical artist only on occasion.[10]

From the beginning, it could be argued (and Williams goes on to do so) Parker just *blew*. As I remarked in Part One, nothing seemed to affect his ability to do this sublimely and with a perfect grasp of form and content. But that is not the full story. Parker's own solos may all be monuments to perfection, but they are often sullied – or at least compromised – by their context; in this respect the altoist was far from being blessed. On many occasions his work – coldly considered as *art* in the way that Williams rightly insists upon – was variously impaired by poor recording techniques, inappropriate material (though like Armstrong he could always transcend that), inferior confrères and insufficient pre-planning. In addition, not the least aspect of Parker's tragedy is that he died *when* he did.

By March 1955 the long-playing record was coming decisively into its own. It had been around for several years, but musicians and producers had needed time to understand its full potential. Typically, Norman Granz had grasped it earlier than most: **The Jam Sessions** of July 1952 gave his chosen musicians scope to 'stretch out' in a way both natural to them and almost unheard-of in a recording studio. Those musicians included tenorists Flip Philips and Ben Webster, trumpeter Charlie Shavers, and altoists Benny Carter, Johnny Hodges and Parker, and on *Jam Blues* and *Funky Blues* they are able to play without the kind of time constraint that had hitherto characterised recording. As one would expect, Parker rises triumphantly to the occasion; partly because it gives an almost unbearably tantalising sense of what might have been, his performances here are amongst his most important.

The Jam Sessions remains a signal achievement, but in one crucial respect it was a thoroughly traditional enterprise. On this occasion Granz used the new technology to preserve for posterity what his stellar personnel in particular and jazz musicians in general had excelled at from the start – unpressured explorations of all kinds of material in congenial company. But the advent of the long-playing record opened up more radical opportunities. Uninterrupted playing times of fifteen minutes and above was a godsend for ambitious writers, for musicians wishing to investigate form in extended fashion, and for producers interested in what these days would be called 'the concept album'.[11]

This expansion was not necessarily all good news, naturally. The 78 rpm record had the virtues of its vices: its very limitations precluded empty volubility and lengthy pretension – two flaws that the long-player could encourage. But it gave the better jazzmen unparalleled scope. Under Teo Macero's aegis at Columbia Miles Davis scaled new heights and Parker's old colleague Dizzy Gillespie was another major beneficiary with Verve. In a way the LP itself was just as much responsible for such triumphs as **Miles Ahead** and **Gillespiana** as were Davis & Gil Evans and Gillespie & Lalo Schifrin.

Few would doubt that Parker would have mined this vast new seam with surpassing flair; the fact is that, his summit meeting with Carter and Hodges excepted, he was never able to do so. And if Martin Williams and my supporting arguments are right, it is possible that future histories of jazz will revise Parker's reputation. No one will gainsay his supreme gifts or his all-pervading influence on modern jazz; neither will it be denied that he had more intuitive talent than any jazzman save Armstrong, Tatum and Bix Beiderbecke. But while generations to come will continue to thrill to the perfection of Parker's solos, they may also deem many of them brilliant fragments or cameos, not fully integrated masterpieces.

It would be idiotic to suggest that the young Rollins of 1949 would have been prescient enough to see that Parker's aesthetic achievement might eventually be compromised in the way outlined. But there were two ways in which he was able to capitalise on technological developments and thus extend his idol's gospel. First, he used the long-player format more imaginatively than almost anyone – as witness the string of albums cut in the late 50s, as notable for their catholicity as for their excellence. Second, his awareness of form was not just intuitively profound: from the outset he took pains to think about and study such matters. The same combination of inspiration and cerebration underscores the strategy Rollins defines in the quotation headlining this chapter, and it leads me to another hybrid – improvisation itself.

A good deal of nonsense is talked about jazz and improvisation. To be sure, much of what happens in jazz is improvised; on the other hand, much of what is best in jazz goes way beyond the superficially impressive ability to 'make it up as one goes along'. There is nothing contemptible about such a facility, but there's nothing *de facto* wonderful about it either, despite this story related by André Previn:

> Horowitz used to play for an encore two arrangements that he made. One was on themes from *Carmen*, the other was *Stars And Stripes For Ever*, and they were really scary – I mean, they were unbel*iev*able; and Horowitz decided he would do *Tea For Two*. And he went and worked for months writing out these phenomenally difficult virtuoso variations on *Tea For Two*, and then he called Art Tatum and asked him up and played them for him. And Art said, "Yeah, terrific. Unbelievably

difficult." And then he said, "Would you like *me* to play *Tea For Two*?" And Horowitz said, "Yes." So Tatum then played *Tea For Two* until Horowitz stopped him – I mean, he just went on and on and on. And Horowitz said, "When did you figure all that out?" And Tatum said, "Well, just now." And that of course is the big trick and the big secret.[12]

Few people are as intelligent about music (classical or jazz) as Previn, but here he advances two highly questionable claims. First, the notion that "unbelievably difficult" is *per se* an aesthetic criterion will not do. Technical virtuosity is only meaningful as a means to an end, and Philip Larkin is right to insist that "Technique by itself is as boring in jazz as anywhere else."[13] Second – and central to my overall argument – I think Previn was mistaken in suggesting that Tatum's readings of *Tea For Two* were superior to Horowitz's simply because the former were *extempore* and the latter written down and arduously revised. If they *were* better, that might have had more to do with the qualities of Tatum's musical mind than with the mere fact of spontaneity.

Previn's further contention that spontaneous invention is jazz's definitive strength – "the big trick and the big secret" – also requires examination. Some of the finest jazz contains little or no improvisation. One thinks immediately of many Ellington works – *Harlem Air Shaft, Tone Parallel To Harlem, Diminuendo And Crescendo In Blue* (1937 version) and large sections of such works as *Suite Thursday, La Plus Belle Africaine, Black And Tan Fantasy* and *Rockin' In Rhythm*. In all those (and more) Ellington mines the unique gifts of the musicians then in his band, endowing the works with a special immediacy rarely found outside jazz; however, the amount of extempore exploration is slight indeed. Significantly, the arrangement of *Rockin' In Rhythm* – including the solos – changed hardly at all across the fifty years it was performed; it's also worth noting, with reference to Previn's Tatum-Horowitz story, that when asked why he always played *Tea For Two* the same way, Tatum replied, "Because I don't know a better way of playing it."

And that, to return to a point telegraphed in Part One, is one of the reasons why "the sound of surprise" is a wholly inadequate definition of jazz. Whitney Balliett never writes less than very well – in the words of one admirer, he "brings jazz journalism to the verge of poetry"[14] – but his ears are often less impressive than his prose. His insights tend to be precious rather than valuable, largely because his governing view of the music is reductive and condescending:

> Jazz is, after all, a highly personal, lightweight form ... that, shaken down, amounts to the blues, some unique vocal and instrumental sounds, and the limited, elusive genius of improvisation ... At best, these can provoke an intense, sometimes profound emotional satisfaction, which is altogether different – largely because of sheer mathematical proportions – from that induced by the design and mass of, say, Berlioz's *Requiem*.[15]

Well, *of course* it's different: the point is not worth making, especially as it ignores all that jazz does do that the *Requiem* does not. Balliett's definitions take no account of jazz as 'America's true classical music"[16] or as "the History of the Negro in music";[17] they make no mention of its profound spiritual and cerebral appeal; above all they ignore *swing*. That unique rhythmic élan is the DNA of jazz, and something which will not be found in the entire classical repertoire.

The criterion of "surprise" has one virtue: it pin-points the awed excitement that every jazz enthusiast will remember feeling when s/he first heard 'the real thing'. But that isn't why one returns again and again to one's favourite records. Nostalgia may play a small part; renewed delight in that rhythmic power and deep satisfaction in formal craftsmanship are considerably more instrumental.

Balliett's criterion is simplistic enough from the point of view of a listener. But in its tendency to confuse logic with predictability and mere spontaneity with value, it also does serious disservice to *musicians* and the way nearly all of them actually operate. Experienced musical judgment and necessarily painstaking thinking are as much a part of great jazz as the inspiration of the moment. The MJQ, rightly lauded for restoring a significant degree of collective improvisation to jazz, played music that was also – indeed simultaneously – very tightly arranged and thought out. And other major combos evince the same reliance on proven arrangements, dedicated planning and absolute musical thoroughness: Miles Davis's Quintets in the 50s & 60s; the astounding Coltrane Quartet; any and all of Oscar Peterson's trios. The pianist recalls how fanatically Ray Brown and Herb Ellis practised:

> They played together in the daytime, apart from the gig, practising harmonic movement. And not set up. They didn't say, "On bar 4 we're going to do this." They practised *possibles*. All the possibles, all the alternatives. And whatever triggering mechanisms they had, they could go any given way at any given time, and they had a way of letting me know which. It was just automatic with them.[18]

The paradox is unimprovable: such "automatic" suppleness and creativity has to be fiercely worked at, has to be *earned*.

Rollins fits into this debate in the neatest way possible. He is a great improviser, consistently audacious and sometimes almost magically imaginative. But he is also a highly cerebral artist, endlessly looking for ways to ensure that his improvisations will work. The idea that Rollins has ever just picked up his horn and strolled breezily onto the bandstand hoping for the best is farcical; if anything, as I've suggested along the way, his problem has at times been that he's thought too much, become too worried about the value of what he was doing, and did not trust his spontaneous flair enough. Maybe that is why he developed such an antipathy for the studio – and that brings me to the last general point I want to make on the subject of Rollins the master-improviser.

When observing in the Preface that many critics have drawn attention to the difference between Rollins in concert and Rollins in record, I suggested that two issues were involved – the particular case of Rollins himself but also the abiding tension in jazz itself between 'live' spontaneity and organised preservation. I address the latter first.

Many jazz musicians have expressed a dislike of the recording studio. That is hardly surprising. Warm and communicative by nature, jazz thrives on rapport and (my remarks above notwithstanding) spontaneity – all of them properties hardly endemic to an environment dominated by booths, microphones and anti-septic dutifulness. Oscar Peterson spoke for many artists, I'm sure, when he observed:

> I've never greatly cared for studios: they're cold, and I find that tough. Obviously, there's no audience to strike up a rapport with, and aside from that, riding up in an elevator to the tenth floor sure is second best to going on stage. That makes it hard to reach your best level of playing.[19]

On the other hand, any suggestion that live work is always superior to studio performance would be absurd whoever the musician, and I offer five major examples in proof. The studio work of Miles Davis during the 50s and 60s is the equal of anything he did in concert; many would argue that (say) **Miles Ahead, Kind of Blue** and **ESP** are superior. The triple-peaked apogee of 40s big band jazz – Ellington's **The Blanton-Webster Band**, Gillespie's **Complete RCA-Victor Recordings** and Woody Herman's **Thundering Herds**[20] – were all studio recordings. The post-MJQ work in the 1970s of Milt Jackson offers a further corrective. His concert performances at Montreux in 1975 were admittedly superb – he was by common consent the star of the Festival – but they are no more compelling than such studio dates as **The Big 3** with Ray Brown & Joe Pass or the marvellous albums those three together with Mickey Roker recorded as Quadrant. And to return to Peterson himself: the string of studio

Verves he cut with Ray Brown and Ed Thigpen in the early 60s are every bit as fine as that group's live work; indeed, many (including me) think the December 1962 **Night Train** the pianist's finest hour.

Peterson is as conscientious a jazz musician as there has ever been, but no more so than Rollins. It is the *manner* of their perfectionism which differs, adroitly glossed by someone who had a high regard for both of them as men and musicians – Ronnie Scott:

> ... There are as many attitudes and conceptions of, and manners of, improvisation, and ways of working with improvisation, as there are people. Oscar Peterson, for instance, is a very, very polished, technically immaculate, performer who, I hope he wouldn't mind me saying so, trots out these fantastic things that he has perfected and it really is a remarkable performance. Whereas Sonny Rollins, he could go on one night and maybe it's disappointing, and another night he'll just take your breath away by his kind of imagination and so forth. And it would be different every night with Rollins.[21]

Such "attitudes" also inform their approach to recording. However deflating Peterson may still find the confines of the studio, he has in different vein also called it 'The Proving Ground'[22]. The inference is that he will always do his utmost to ensure as professional and satisfying a performance as possible: he is a man of great pride (in the best sense) and iron will. But no matter how much Rollins may have wished to emulate such consistency, both his natural diffidence and ingrained dislike of the recording process made it increasingly difficult for him to do so, and I think one has to concede that 'studio-block' really did affect him in the end.

The crucial question, however, is *when*: at what stage did his studio work show a marked and regular inferiority to his in-person performances? For Martin Williams the discrepancy had become decisive by 1962. In *The Jazz Tradition* he quotes his review of a Rollins concert in that year, part of which reads –

> Rollins's final piece was a kind of extemporaneous orchestration on *If Ever I Would Leave You* in which he became brass, reed, and rhythm section, tenor soloist, and Latin percussionist, all at once and always with musical logic.

- and then adds:

> Again, one is left with frustration that Rollins's recordings do not show the level of his achievements in clubs and concerts. There is a recording of *If Ever I Would Leave You*; it is very good indeed, but it is a shadow of the masterful performance described above.[23]

And Dave Gelly wrote of a 1993 concert:

> He turns tunes inside-out, takes them to pieces, reassembles them back-to-front, gives them a good shaking up and after about 10 minutes they reappear, bewildered but undamaged. It is done wholeheartedly, with wit and enormous affection, and the effect is overpowering.
>
> Much of this comes over on record, but with nothing like the potency ... This was the best Rollins I have heard for at least 15 years.[24]

Having as a young man caught Rollins at Ronnie Scott's in 1965 and as a middle-aged one shared the "inspirational experience" of that 1993 concert, I would echo both critics' words.* But I cannot agree that any such discrepancy is evident during his first decade. With the exception of the live dates performed by the Brown-Roach Quintet, all Rollins's best work of that period was recorded in a studio. The 1957 Village Vanguard sessions fascinate, but as I argued in Part One, they are not wholly successful.

* (see also CODA, pages 174-176)

No matter that Rollins called his 50s work "promiscuous" and that he recorded for a raft of labels and producers: the result in virtually every case was music that warrants the adjective 'mighty'. Since his 1959 sabbatical, that word cannot often be applied to his studio work – certain performances for RCA, almost all of **On Impulse!**, and a good deal of **Sunny Days, Starry Nights** and **Plus 3**, but not much more. This may be very unfair on Orrin Keepnews in particular, a man of great honour and insight; the fact is that a lot of Rollins's records from 1962 onwards have either a febrile or a routine quality that never occurred when he was leaping from Prestige to Riverside to Contemporary to Verve and points south.

In the last analysis, however, Rollins's records will be his only tangible legacy – and as I hope I've demonstrated along the way, all but a handful of them will continue to illuminate and satisfy. And even they do not quite tell the whole story, they amply document the three other key constituents of his art I end by addressing: his predilection for the calypso and swinging 'good-time music'; his fondness for odd-ball tunes; and the spirituality which has a political dimension as well.

Rollins's love of the calypso reflects his West Indian heritage; it also embodies another paradox inherent in his musical nature. Ostensibly casual, spontaneous and light-hearted, its form is in fact the result of evolutionary refinement and epitomises an entire culture. As such, it is both highly organised and wonderfully elastic. There's a natural bouncing lift to the calypso that speaks deeply to Rollins's taste for dance rhythms, his instinctive swing and his liking for accessible melodies; on the other hand, its dense formal properties facilitate some of his most penetrating and challenging improvisations. [A similarly deceptive simplicity informs the blues, of course: it is no accident that Rollins is one of the finest blues players ever.] And if the 1956 *St Thomas* remains the definitive expression of this heady amalgam, many subsequent forays confirm the wisdom of his commitment to the genre. As noted, *Don't Stop The Carnival* has been the cornerstone of his concert performances for twenty years, often in performances that extend beyond twenty minutes, and the Milestone albums feature a hatful of calypso-type numbers. Such devotion suggests a man who has come to regard the calypso's virile litheness with the particular affection one always has for something which serves one best.

That fondness confirms another central quality. Rollins *swings*. He swings effortlessly and instinctively: even at his most jagged or awkward, that rhythmic pulse always asserts itself, rescuing his least fine performances and making the greatest ones even more sublime. Nowhere is this more evident than on those calypsos, whose lissom warmth and muscular snap are the perfect correlatives for his ambitious yet down-home art.

Rollins's taste for unusual material manifested itself early on and has been a consistent feature of his repertoire. His *oeuvre* contains a string of titles which no other jazzman has recorded or probably thought of recording: a random half dozen might include *There's No Business Like Show Business* (1956), *Rock-A-Bye Your Baby* and *If You Were The Only Girl In The World* (1958), *You Are My Lucky Star* (1964), *We Kiss In A Shadow* (1966) and *Swing Low, Sweet Chariot* (1974)[25].

Several explanations have been advanced for such choices. The one I have least time for now (though I confess I went along with it once) is that Rollins wishes to draw sneering attention to these tunes' awfulness, thereby commenting on the impoverishment of Tin Pan Alley and its devotees. The idea does not square with his essentially gentle nature or his wide-ranging aesthetic grasp. More important still, it does not explain why his treatment of the material is invariably so joyous. There is a degree of affectionate lampoon in what he does with them, but it is underscored by respect for the songs' musical possibilities – nowhere more evident than on **Way Out West**. *I'm An Old Cowhand* and *Wagon Wheels* are rich in a genial humour that is on the side of the material, never contemptuous of it. It is surely apt that "Way Out West" was also the title of one of Laurel and Hardy's most inspired films: the same anarchic but loving humour informs the work of Rollins, Brown and Manne, in which the material is approached transcendentally rather than with scorn.

Perhaps the best example of this side of him is *Toot Toot Tootsie* (on **The Sound Of Sonny**). The tune was made famous by Al Jolson, and one might imagine that his blacked-up antics offended Rollins at a fundamental level, as they arguably must offend all blacks. Yet it should be remembered that Jolson was a Jew, and one can infer from his knowing humour a sardonic awareness of the prejudice and hatred which minorities of all kinds could attract. All that would have appealed to Rollins's angular wit, and his reading of the tune is notable for its virile good spirits. Indeed, his enjoyment is as immense as it obvious: one can almost see him grinning at the outrage or earnest puzzlement the choice of tune might occasion in some circles as he drolly clips the melody round the ear and wades into its potential with delighted gusto.

Rollins's *penchant* for singular material material and attendant humour are also a reminder of three other features of his art and personality. First, they underline his kinship with Lester Young, whose idiosyncratic wit is hardly less renowned than his tenor playing. Young found a lot of things amusing, including many songs; like Rollins, however, he treated them fondly and with respect – as witness his conversance with their lyrics, no matter how superficially trivial they may have seemed. He also understood how rhythmically enabling such material could prove, and it was a lesson Rollins learned early: quite apart from anything else about them, *Toot Toot Tootsie* and *Rock-A-Bye Your Baby* swing irresistibly. Second, and closely related to the first, it is another paradox that Rollins the archetypal modernist should turn with such imaginative affection to the 'corny' tunes of the distant past: 'Sonny Plays Jolson' seems positively oxymoronic. However, a genuine oxymoron expresses not a contradiction but a synthesis, and that is the case here – another instance of Rollins creatively combining the best of two worlds.

The third feature dramtised is the wide gulf in approach between Rollins and John Coltrane. The latter, obsessive enough even in his days with Miles Davis[26], became more and more *driven.* His search for the ultimate musical and spiritual truth grew yearly in intensity and – who knows? – may have hastened his demise. Coltrane was and remains a towering figure in jazz, but listening to his music there are times when I'm reminded of Eric Morecombe's appraisal of *For Whom The Bell Tolls*: "Not many laughs in that."

Some observers have found Rollins analogously intense,[27] and there are certainly occasions – at every stage of his career – when he can seem a man possessed. But not only is his humour never far away: it is all-informing even when it is dormant or only implicit. Through humour, Rollins found another way of extending his musical and emotional range. Others to have done this include Fats Waller, violinist Stuff Smith and – at a lower level but still significant – Rollins's original inspiration Louis Jordan. Pre-eminent amongst this 'type' is of course Dizzy Gillespie: no wonder he and Rollins collaborated so successfully.

My final focus is the spiritual and political dimension of Rollins's work and life. As explored in Part One, the early years of his career coincided with bleak and often tawdry developments in the USA that made sad nonsense of the hopes that had burned so brightly at the end of World War II. Particularly dispiriting was the paralysis which gripped the cause of Civil Rights, a failure which many American blacks – Rollins amongst them – regarded as wilful. Never a political activist in any flag-waving way, he was both idealistic enough to believe that jazz had shown what *could* be done and well enough versed in America's ways to recognise the depth and scale of opposition to such advances. I have already quoted the remarks that follow, but I make no apology for that:

they are worth repeating anyway, and they could not be more germane to **The Freedom Suite**, the one major Rollins *opus* I have not discussed and to which I turn in a moment.

> Jazz was not just a music: it was a social force in this country, and it was talking about freedom and people enjoying things for what they are and not having to worry about whether they were supposed to be black, white and all that stuff. Jazz has always been a music that had that kind of spirit. Now I believe that for that reason the people who *could* push jazz have *not* pushed jazz, because that's what jazz means. A lot of times, jazz means no barriers.

To Rollins music has always been a source of potential enlightenment, of human growth, of bringing people together in harmony and pleasure; that may indeed be why he chose to pursue a career in jazz. In this respect he resembles Stevie Wonder, whose great wealth has not diluted his visceral commitment to better times; I find it warmingly appropriate that Rollins has recorded some of Wonder's work, even if the musical results are only partially satisfying.

In the words of producer Orrin Keepnews, **The Freedom Suite** was "Sonny's first venture into extended composition."[28] Unless one counts **Alfie** or the 1985 **Solo Album**, it was also his last, and were there no other considerations it would occupy a special place in his *oeuvre*. But it also marked his last significant partnership with Max Roach and perhaps the most sustained attempt at collective improvisation he ever undertook; in addition, it quickly became controversial in a fashion unlike any Rollins record before or since. At the same time it encapsulates much of what is central to Rollins's style and achievement. It is highly sophisticated music that nonetheless swings hard and is richly melodic. Its political overtness is more pronounced than in other Rollins work but adumbrates his overall vision, and its compositional rigour is the apotheosis of his writing flair. All in all, it is a suitable work with which to close my account.

The Freedom Suite has four main themes. The first is simple enough, eight bars in length, but Sonny's exploration quicks grows in intensity and complexity, lightened by a sudden quotation from *The Donkey Serenade* while growing organically as a single structure rather than as a series of choruses based on given chords. The second, in waltz-time, is a beautifully-balanced series of individual 'lead' performances which are always subservient to the structural whole; even Rollins's superb closing cadenza is no more (and no less) than a virtuoso re-examination of the theme's essential properties. The third theme, rightly dubbed "Ellingtonish" by Charles Fox[29], at one point reintroduces the previous waltz-motif, played exactly as it was before, heightening one's sense of the suite's deep structure; the quotations from *Easy Living* are equally apposite. The final theme at times nudges towards the harmonies of *Lover Come Back To Me*, but, more centrally pertinent, it is an up-tempo reworking of the opening tune. Some of Rollins's playing here recalls *I Know That You Know* in its blistering intensity, but the celebration of hard bop is ultimately secondary to its function as a climactic reprise of the **Suite**'s controlling ideas.

The composition as a whole is beautifully rounded, both metaphorically and literally: the final phrase echoes the first, illustrating Sartre's observation that one can infer the ending of many great works of art from what is laid down in their first moments. (Making the same point, Charles Fox quotes T.S.Eliot's "In my end is my beginning" from *East Coker*.[30]) But neither such formal considerations – wonderfully realised though they are – nor the many moments of wistful beauty can entirely account for the **Suite**'s power; to do full justice to its yearning tenderness one has to look beyond formal musical criteria.

On the 1958 sleeve Rollins wrote:

> America is deeply rooted in Negro culture: its colloquialisms, its humour, its music. How ironic that the Negro, who more than any other people can claim America's culture as his own,

> is being persecuted and repressed, that the Negro, who has exemplified the humanities in his very existence, is being rewarded with inhumanity.

Intelligent, temperate and in my view unanswerably *right*, those words at once caused a *furore* that prompted Riverside to pull the album off the market and reissue it as **Shadow Waltz,** the title of the second-shortest piece on the album. One would call the irony delicious were it not so depressing: such a reaction proved – devastatingly – the point that inspired **The Freedom Suite** in the first place and thereby exemplified so much of what was nationally amiss.

And although things may have moved on somewhat since then, there is still a long long way to go. Rollins may well have wanted to believe that music "is a beautiful way of bringing people together, a little bit of an oasis in this messed-up world," as he put it to Art Taylor in 1971[31]; however, other things, other people and other squalid and cowardly prejudices keep getting in the way. At least he is in very good company; I shall shortly be quoting three other distinguished jazzmen on the reception of jazz in its own land, but first some words written in 1893.

> I am now satisfied that the future music of this country must be founded on what are called the negro melodies. This must be the real foundation of any serious and original school of composition to be developed in the United States.[32]

The author is Antonin Dvorak, who in May of that year completed his 'New World' Symphony #9 in E minor, dedicated to America itself. Right from the start, however, much of twentieth-century America was against Dvorak's prognosis in general and jazz in particular, as witness these anonymous remarks of 1924 –

> Jazz, especially when it depends on that ghastly instrument, the saxophone, offends people with musical taste already formed, and it prevents the formation of musical tastes by others.[33]

– or this denunciation by Sigmund Spaeth, which despite resembling an attack on the New Thing of the 60s, dates from 1928:

> Merely a raucous and inarticulate shouting of hoarse-throated instruments, with each player trying to outdo his fellows in fantastic cacophony.[34]

Just as Presley would do fifty years later, jazz thrilled some and alarmed and disgusted others. Unlike Presley, serious jazz musicians were not prepared to compromise. That is to their immense and permanent credit, but it explains why the noes came to have it, as these magisterial reflections sadly confirm.

> I'm hardly surprised that my kind of music is still without, let us say, official honour at home. Most Americans still take it for granted that European music – classical music, if you will – is the only really respectable kind. *[Angrily]* What we do, what other black musicians do, has always been like the kind of man you wouldn't want your daughter to associate with.
>
> Duke Ellington[35]

> America did invent *an entire musical form* – jazz; it seems to me that almost from the outset it was suppressed by the racist American white who would have no part of this 'jungle music'... Even more remarkable – and distressing – has been Western blacks' acquiescence in this process.
>
> Oscar Peterson[36]

And as the curtest possible summary:

> Jazz is too good for Americans.
>
> Dizzy Gillespie[37]

I suppose there are some who would dismiss Rollins, Ellington, Peterson and Gillespie as a quartet of bitter paranoiacs looking for an excuse for their own failures. Others will not only understand their anger and recognise the grim truths spoken; they will recall that none of the four gave up trying despite such deep feelings of betrayal. Ellington and Gillespie continued to work right up to their deaths; Peterson and Rollins are still heroically active in the autumn of their lives. All four are exemplars of Romanticism at its most stirring, and it is with Rollins the Romantic artist that I close.

One of the best definitions of Romantic zeal was coined by Norman Mailer in his 1962 essay 'Ten Thousand Words A Minute':

> To believe the impossible may be won creates a strength from which the impossible may indeed be attacked.[38]

Rollins's Romanticism may not be as strenuous as Mailer's, but it is no less profound. A musician of supreme gifts, there were times when he thought – as do all serious Romantic artists – that his work could make a decisive difference to America and the world at large. He wanted to realise through and in his music the better times he and millions of others wanted (The same idealism characterises the 'Green' preoccupation of his very latest album, **Global Warming**). Nobody would blame him for not succeeding – failure goes with the territory when your pursuit is the impossible; but it is instructive to consider in summary the reasons why he has not been able to deliver all that he hoped to.

First, there are the contradictions inherent in Romanticism and in jazz itself that I have already discussed – the synthesising conflict between old and new, between conservative and radical, between formal planning and spontaneity, and between art and making a living. Second, there are the inner contradictions in the man himself – the supreme improviser who felt progressively more constrained in a studio; the artist dedicated both to experiment and to spiritual oneness who could nonetheless never accept the self-subsumation as a player or the intrinsic narcissim that seemed to require; the Rollins who loved good time music but who often seemed to go out of his way to make life difficult both for himself and his audience. And third and most definitive, there is his diffidence, allied to an endearing old-fashionedness.

"I don't have the greatest opinion of myself,"[40] Rollins told Art Taylor[40]. As I've observed from the start, it seems hard to reconcile that kind of admission with the tumultuous authority of so much of his playing, but that 1971 remark does help to explain certain important aspects of his art and career. Nobody could be less of a dilettante, yet there are several things Rollins never explored with the kind of full-bloodedness one might have expected – the ways paved by the avant garde; the advent of the bossa nova; regular partnership with a front-line partner of equal stature; the use of the soprano saxophone; the drone properties of the tenor; and the use of multi-dubbing and other developments in recording technology. All such possibilities required a fibre-deep confidence he did not have or an unalloyed belief he could not find.

Another way of expressing the same point is to suggest that his deepest impulses are timeless rather than modern. The great blues player; the irresistible swinger; the natural melodist; the inspired communicator; those characteristics not only define the core of Rollins's art and achievement but just happen to enshrine the fundamental truths of jazz. It is surely significant – indeed, I would say it is positively symbolic – that his best latter-day album features a regal exploration of Jerome Kern's *I'm Old Fashioned.*[40] Rollins is and always has been a more conservative artist than some of the more spectacular aspects of his career might indicate, and for my final exhibits in defence of that contention I turn to his two 1950s recordings of *Body And Soul.*

The first, briefly mentioned earlier, is to be found on **Max Roach Plus Four** (Emarcy). It was recorded just three months after

Clifford Brown's death, and the quintet performs with almost overwhelming threnodic force. It is far from unrelievedly mournful, however: Kinny Dorham's playing reminds one of the affirmative zeal of Brownie's life and art; solos from Ray Bryant and bassist George Morrow are as melodious as heartfelt; and Rollins's statement of the melody is classically perfect as well as drenched in emotion. His subsequent solo is similarly conservative. The anonymous sleeve essayist calls his closing cadenza "startling", but that's not really true: its beauty and impact are utterly in keeping with everything that has gone before. The reading has an organic logic that characterises all the finest jazz.

Just under two years later Rollins revisited *Body And Soul* as a solo feature. (It is the final track on **Trio/Brass.**) It is a bold performance but wholly accessible: the tenorist's variations are rhythmic rather than harmonic, and although the listener needs to concentrate hard, s/he is never in danger of becoming lost. The song comes newly alive but is also newly endorsed – a combination which can be seen as the epitome of Rollins's art.

These two performances serve another purpose. *Body And Soul* is of course ineluctibly associated with Coleman Hawkins, whose 1939 version is "one of the most celebrated improvisations in music."[41] That remark comes from Gary Giddins's fascinating survey 'Fifty Years of *Body And Soul*'; he does not cite Rollins's earlier version but says of the 1958 solo performance

> Though the playing is often magnificent, a comparison with the abstractions of Hawkins's *Picasso* makes the Old Man look godlike. [42]

I sense that Giddins admires this Rollins version less than I do, but no matter: his comparison is expertly judged. His previous sentence contains the observation "Rollins turned to tradition", which is not just apposite in this particular case but resonant in a much broader way too. Hawkins's *Body And Soul* may well have been “a gauntlet tossed at every other saxophonist in jazz”[43], but it was as sound and logical as it was incomparable. That combination distinguishes all Rollins’s greatest recordings: he never forgot the defining lessons Hawkins taught him, nor the desire to emulate his first and most enduring Master’s timeless authority. And whereas Hawkins was almost a shell of a man in his last years – by the time of his death at the age of 63 he had dwindled almost literally to nothing, as John Chilton has documented in heart-rending fashion[44] – Rollins has lasted wonderfully well. As he draws near to his seventieth birthday it is clear from both the state of his health and the commanding authority of his playing that, regrettable though some of those ‘missed opportunities’ may seem at times, he was right to stay true to what he was and remains – a colossus of the tenor saxophone.

CODA

On April 24, 1982 I was at Ronnie Scott's Club to catch the last of four nights by 'The Quartet' – a majestic outfit comprising Mickey Roker, Ray Brown, pianist Monty Alexander and Milt Jackson. Their two sets contained some of the finest jazz I ever expect to hear,[45] and one of the selections was Brown's composition *FSR*. That decodes as 'For Sonny Rollins', and it was indeed a crystalline evocation of the tenorist's phrasing and swaggering attack. Three of the four men have made triumphant recordings in Rollins's company, and I hope there is still time for Alexander to do so. The pianist adores Rollins's work, having once said, "Sonny can go out there and just play melody and still fracture me"[46], and his own inspirational feel for the calypso form would alone make them an ideal pairing. But my chief reason for citing *FSR* and including this coda is that its irresistible swing and muscular joy epitomised almost everything that is greatest in Rollins's improvising. Over and above all the challenges he sets, the complexities he explores and the questions he asks, Rollins's music at its affirmative best simply makes one glad to be alive.

That sentence was to have been my last one. However, it took on a massive extra resonance on April 18, 1998 when, a few days after completing the manuscript, I saw Rollins at London's Barbican. He was accompanied by Clifton Anderson, Stephen Scott, Bob Cranshaw, drummer Perry Wilson and percussionist Victor See-Yuen, and it was one of the finest concerts I have ever attended. Rollins looked in ridiculously good shape for a man nearing his seventies, and the series of marathon performances that ensued was a testament to his stamina, as indeed were his p-a announcements, delivered with warmth, wit and not a trace of breathlessness! He looked – and played – like an athlete, confirming all over again Freddie Hubbard's masterly aperçus of 1966:

> Some of the quality of [Sonny's] tone is due to the strength of his body. He knows how to get the right amount of air into his horn and he has the strength to keep it coming and to control

> it. He always had a deep sound, and he learned how to perfect that depth of sound all over the instrument, from top to bottom.[47]

The sextet struck me as the best outfit Rollins has had for ages. Scott was superb throughout; See-Yuen's imaginative and pulsating effects recalled Rollins's partnership with the great Mtume in the 70s; and Wilson was a revelation – as *sympathique* a drummer as Rollins has had since those days with Roach. There were three glorious calypsos, stirring readings of Berlin's *They Say It's Wonderful*, and Ellington's *In A Sentimental Mood*, and several selections from Rollins's new CD, **Global Warming**: *Clear-Cuttin' Boogie* was a particular triumph. Perhaps *the* highspot, though, was the tenorist's solo-deconstruction-&-re-assembly of *A Nightingale Sang In Berkeley Square*, a ten-minute tour de force of astounding power, melodic invention, humour and structural insight, brilliantly rounded off via the opening progression of *Sophisticated Lady*.

Nevertheless, I was expecting something along those lines, even if it eclipsed previous experiences. What I wasn't prepared for was the colossal power of his playing. Towards the end of the closing *Don't Stop The Carnival* he produced two or three blistering choruses in a register that I thought belonged only to the bass saxophone. One has heard the odd such note in performances by Stan Getz and Rollins himself, but not sustained in this way and with such ferocious rhythmic authority. And even when exploring the tenor's more conventional properties, Rollins's sound had the force of a tidal wave: I'm sure I was far from alone in feeling light-headed for hours afterwards.

There was one poignant aspect to an otherwise transcendental evening, best introduced by re-quoting a sentence from Dave Gelly's review of that 1993 Drury Lane gig:

> Much of this comes over on record, but with nothing like the potency.[48]

The Barbican concert resurrected the question that has bewildered so many Rollins enthusiasts these thirty years: *why*? Why can't he produce this kind of music when recording? And I'm not simply re-heating earlier observations concerning Rollins in the studio. As Orrin Keepnews pointed out in suitably vinegary tones a long time ago, the problem is both deeper and broader:

> Every so often a really clever writer comes up with The Answer: since Rollins is unhappy in the studio, even a record producer should know enough to capture him in actual club or concert performance! The only trouble with this idea is that Sonny is nobody's fool; he can easily recognise recording microphones and tape machines wherever he sees them, and nothing much is gained by turning a nightclub or concert hall into a recording-studio-with-audience. I know: I've tried it a couple of times.[49]

The Cutting Edge was a wondrous exception to that rather baleful summary, as is *Powaii* on the JVC album **Live In Japan**, but exceptions they remain, and the sad possibility is that some of the greatest things Rollins ever did will have no memorial save in the neural traces of those who were there at the time. But if (as now seems beyond all argument) the concert hall is the only *milieu* that brings out his consummate genius to the full, I just hope that someone, somewhere doesn't give up on the idea of preserving the results for posterity. For – to repeat what were to have been my last words – Rollins's music at its affirmative best simply makes one glad to be alive. That may not be the most earnest testament one can pay to an artist, but as far as I'm concerned it is the most eloquent.

Richard Palmer Bedford, England, April 1998

Notes

1 Alan Munton, 'Misreading Morrison, Mishearing Jazz: A Response to Toni Morrison's Jazz Critics', *Journal of American Studies*, xxxi (1997), 251.

2 Advanced by Alan J. Rice in his 'Jazzin' It Up A Storm: The Execution and Meaning of Toni Morrison's Jazzy Prose Style', *Journal of American Studies*, xxviii (1994), 424.

3 Munton, 243. He further points out that "The same sequence of theme and solos occurs in all versions," as established by Thomas Owens in his essay 'Forms' in *The New Grove Dictionary of Jazz.*

4 Munton, 244.

5 *Ibid*, 244. Munton also deftly observes that both Rodgers's original song and the Coltrane Quartet's versions of it are in 3/4, "a time signature that does not occur in African drumming."

6 On the 1989 sleeve essay accompanying **Louis Armstrong Volume IV - Louis Armstrong And Earl Hines,** CBS 466308-2.

7 See above, page 37.

8 Collier, 453.

9 When Oscar Peterson launched his Advanced School of Contemporary Music in Toronto in 1960 (in harness with Ray Brown, Ed Thigpen and Canadian clarinetist & composer Phil Nimmons), his 'Ur-text' for students was Young's work with Nat 'King' Cole. He was convinced that the simplicity of their lines and the quality of their time were models for all aspirants, regardless of their approach or idiom: "First of all, if (that music) doesn't reach you, you're in trouble; but if it does reach you and you can't come up with that in some shape or form, you're not going to get very far." [In conversation with André Previn; see Note 12 below.]

10 ed. Horricks, *These Jazzmen Of Our Time* (London, Gollancz, 1960), 199-200.

11 Granz himself had taken the initiative in this area with the ten albums Oscar Peterson recorded between 1952 and 1954. Known generically as the **Songbooks** series, each was dedicated to an outstanding exponent of the American popular song - Gershwin, Arlen, Rodgers and so on. The project was an artistic triumph but it was – and remains – widely misunderstood. Many Peterson fans were disappointed by the lack of developed

improvisation, failing to realise that the pianist and his colleagues were in these instances concerned with the composers' art, not their own. [Any reader interested in exploring this music further is referred to my 1996 compilation for Verve, **The Song Is You: The Best Of The Oscar Peterson Songbooks** (2CD 314 531 558-2); Verve plan eventually to issue all the albums in discrete form.] Fortunately, Granz was not deterred by the jazz public's lukewarm response to the Peterson project; soon would follow the related – and hugely successful – **Ella Fitzgerald Songbooks.**

12 André Previn in conversation with Oscar Peterson, *Omnibus*, BBC-tv, screened in December 1974.

13 *All What Jazz*, 151. That said, I do warm to the reply Segovia gave when asked after a concert why he had played a certain piece so fast: "Because I can."

14 The admirer was himself a poet – Philip Larkin in *All What Jazz*, 212.

15 *The Sound Of Surprise*, 9.

16 See above, Part One, Note 59.

17 Tony Crombie, in *Jazz at Ronnie Scott's*, 179.

18 Lees 128-9.

19 In private conversation with the author in The Hague, 1991. Peterson's remarks echo those written thirty-five years earlier for the sleeve note of **The Oscar Peterson Trio At The Stratford Shakespeare Festival** (now on Verve 314, 513 752-2): "Many ... have felt that the delicate and communicative rapport that they sensed at our in-person performances was usually lost in the mechanical and cold confines of a recording studio. I am inclined to agree that our group performs much better ... (when) a live audience is involved."

20 The Ellington is on RCA 5659 -2 (3-CD), the Gillespie on RCA 07863 66528-2 (2CD) and the Herman on Columbia C3L 25 (3LP).

21 Quoted in Derek Bailey, *Improvisation: Its Nature and Practice in Music* (Ashbourne: Moorland, 1980), 67.

22 In private conversation with the author, Canada, 1994.

23 *The Jazz Tradition*, 191-2.

24 *The Observer*, October 24, 1993.

25 Although *Swing Low, Sweet Chariot* is an important P.D.

spiritual, I cannot think of any other determined modernist who has used it. The only semi-exception is Dizzy Gillespie, who adapted it for his *Swing Low, Sweet Cadillac*. As I point out shortly in the main text, Rollins and Gillespie are a lot closer in spirit – especially in their humour – than might readily be imagined, so these separate recordings are not without extra-musical significance.

26 It is related that an anguished Coltrane confided in Davis about his inability to stop playing once his solos reached a certain level of intensity. "Try taking the saxophone out of your mouth," the trumpeter replied.

27 Whitney Balliett spoke in the mid-50s of his "persistently goatlike tone" and thought that "his solos often resemble endless harangues" (*The Sound Of Surprise*, 68 & 48). Neither judgment matches my own experience of Rollins's work at the time, though the first could perhaps be applied to some of his 60s performances.

28 On the sleeve notes to Riverside 258 LP.

29 On the sleeve notes to **The Freedom Suite Plus**, a double-LP released in the UK on Milestone 47007. Fox's essay is masterly throughout and is required reading.

30 *Ibid*.

31 Arthur Taylor, *Notes And Tones: Musician-To-Musician Interviews* (London: Quartet, 1983), 172.

32 Antonin Dvorak, 'Real Value of Negro Melodies', *New York Herald*, 21 May, 1893.

33 Editorial, *New York Times*, October 8, 1924.

34 Spaeth's essay was entitled 'Jazz Is Not Music'. The extract I quote and other snippets are cited in *All What Jazz*, 159, after which Larkin comments, "It makes you despair of human perception."

35 Duke Ellington speaking to Nat Hentoff in 1965. Quoted in John Edward Hasse, *Beyond Category* (New York: Omnibus, 1995), 397.

36 In a letter to the author, October 1994.

37 Quoted in Jeremy Mitchell & John Pearson, 'Popular Music', *The United States in the Twentieth Century: Culture* (Milton Keynes: The Open University, 1994), 209.

38 Norman Mailer, 'Death', *The Presidential Papers* (London: Deutsch, 1964), 261.

39 Taylor, 169.

40 On *Sunny Days, Starry Nights*.

41 Gary Giddins, 'Fifty Years of Body And Soul', *Rhythm-a-ning*, 48.

42 Ibid, 51.

43 Ibid, 48.

44 John Chilton, *The Song of Hawk: The Life and Recordings of Coleman Hawkins* (London: Quartet, 1990), 366ff.

45 Fortunately, Pablo's engineers were also present, and three CDs preserving music from the four nights have since become available. **Memories of Thelonious Sphere Monk** is on J33J 20055; **A London Bridge** on PACD 2310 932-2; and **Mostly Duke** on PACD 2310 944-2.

46 *Jazz Journal International*, xxxi / i & ii (1978), 15.

47 See Note 55, Part Two.

48 *The Observer*, October 24, 1993.

49 From the booklet accompanying **Sonny Rollins Alternatives**, RCA ND 90651.

© Peter Symes

THREE TRANSCRIPTIONS

I am deeply grateful to Ken Rattenbury for undertaking these transcriptions of *St Thomas, I Know That You Know* and *Three Little Words*. The commentaries accompanying them are also his; my own analysis of the pieces can be found on pages 37-38, 47-48 and 93-94.

R.P.

Not for Rollins those glib corrugations of *arpeggii* sycophantically tracing the basic chord changes which lean perilously close to being no more than technical exercises. Such bland inversions are of no aesthetic consequence, possessing little or no valid compositional substance. Rollins's constructions are a different matter entirely. When examined at leisure, at your own speed, under the microscope of transcription, they reveal sterling passsages of formal development, ingenious embroidery and lyrical depth.

St Thomas

June 22, 1956. Tommy Flanagan (p); Doug Watkins (b); Max Roach (d).

Particular moments to look and listen out for include:

Section 'A' The quirky little motif over Bars 1-8–bouncing between tonic and dominant of the home key–is developed, utilising subtle shifts in syncopation, over the complete section, leading smoothly into the nicely-melodic foray over the next four Bars (9-12).

Section 'B' During Bars 17-20 there is a cutely rearranged reminiscence of the original thoughts expressed over Bars 1-8, then more extended development, cannily rationing the diatonic and the chromatic, to see the section through.

Section 'C' The first eight Bars (33-40) are economical, with plenty of relaxing spaces and a rounded melodic construction that culminates in the neat, simple and no-nonsense phrase in Bars 38 and 39. There is a dash of drama about the sudden excursion into the top register of the tenor saxophone in Bars 41 and 42, relaxing into the decorated scalar descents in Bars 44 to 46 before the passage ends on the mildly imitative Bars 47 and 48.

Section 'D' These two 16-bar sequences show Rollins at his rhythmically extended, lyrical best: smooth, mirrored-melodic constructions (Bar 49, closely recalled by bar 50); the boppish snap of Bar 52; the impassioned flurry of Bar 53, closely followed by the complex syncopations and tidy downward thrusts in Bars 57 and 59; also noteworthy is the belligerently articulated motif in Bar 61. And so it goes on, an aesthetically satisfying miscellany of scalar conservatism, with a garnish of radical but never militant chromaticism enlivening Bars 73 to 76.

In Bar 80, Rollins's crisp lipped-down end-phrase serves to catapult the performance into an extended drum solo where Max Roach contrives, uncharacteristically, to notch up the tempo by several points before Rollins bursts in again at . . .

Section 'F' A fleeting reference to that first motif in the performance occurs during Bars 88 and 89, and those lipped-down keynotes over Bars 94 to 96 are an effectively constructed kick-in to the frenzied flurries which pepper bars 100 and 101 in *Section 'G'*.

Section 'H' Chromatic, adventurous but never anarchic decorations enhance Bars 113 to 120 and, after a dramatic silence, the extreme top end of the instrument is exploited again, to profound effect.

Section 'I' From Bar 129 through to Bar 134, Rollins's smooth quavers are marshalled into groups of six (indicated on the score by the phrase marks), setting up an illusion of 3/4 against basic 4/4 time, pretty close to the old device of secondary ragtime, commonly deployed in that much earlier musical form. Neat!

Section 'J' Rollins's performance draws to a close with (Bar 145) the only sustained use of arpeggiation in this highly concentrated and inventive improvisation.

In all, a remarkable *tour de force*: a scintillating, mercurial and altogether hypnotic demonstration of the art of instant composition.

I Know That You Know

December 19, 1957. Dizzy Gillespie (t); Sonny Stitt (ts); Ray Bryant (p); Tommy Bryant (b); Charlie Persip (d).

After a nicely voiced neo-baroque written introduction for the horns, Dizzy Gillespie, gently supported by the reeds, states the melody of this jaunty song, which is harmonically quite predictable, leaning heavily on the circle-of-fifths progression of related dominants much used in popular song and in jazz composition also. Then, after Bar 30 of the tune, Rollins leaps into the fray with an unaccompanied two-bar lead-in to . . .

Chorus I Straightaway the rhythm trio fractures into stop-time punctuation (on the first beat of every two bars), which is just as well because, freed from the disciplines of a pre-set chordal base, Rollins almost immediately and ingeniously lifts the original B-flat 7th in Bar 3 up a semitone, modulating to E major in Bar 4 before coming on course again in Bar 5, and so on. A similar side-step is negotiated over Bars 12 and 13, where the temporary key change so implied is to D major; later there is another unexpected and highly effective hint of A major in Bars 19 and 20.

It is noticeable, though, that when Rollins encounters the original F 9th chord–as in Bar 1, and looking forward to *Chorus II*, in Bars 33 & 41 and *Chorus III*, Bar 81–he falls back on straight inversions of the harmony, undecorated, with no diminutions or augmentations at all. An exception occurs at Bar 65 in *Chorus III*, where Rollins enters on the F 11th chord, quickly reverting to the plain F 9th. Furthermore, in the tradition of the working composer, Rollins re-uses and develops material which has proved effective at first appearance: compare the skipping, non-syncopated figures in Bars 30 and 31 of *Chorus I* with those appearing over Bars 94 and 95 in *Chorus III*. The notes vary by and large, but the motific and rhythmic reminiscence is easily recognised.

This Rollins creation is notable for its non-outrageous exploration of seemingly unrelated tonalities in the headlong rush of performance, but what is quite outstanding is his effortless, logical and seamless integration of all these surprises into the mainstream of the original sequences. While there is a noticeable chromatic bias throughout, no liberties are taken and not one faltering step. It is a supremely disciplined, well-honed creation, of top-notch quality from start to finish.

Three Little Words

July 8, 1965. Ray Bryant (p); Walter Booker (b); Mickey Roker (d).

For this performance Rollins returned to the highly flexible quartet format; the outcome is a sound and a fury of immense impact and superlative presence. His killer technique makes light of the headlong tempo (a scurrying 84 bars to the minute), his positivity and accuracy a joy to hear. As in many of Rollins's routines, he blasts off with a 10-bar *a capella* (Bars A to F) introduction of such skilful construction that the implied chord sequence is revealed in with crystal clarity, thus: Bars A tp F–3 bars C 7th, followed by single bars of B-flat 7th, A-flat 7th, G-flat 7th. Thereafter in Bars G to J he moves from C to G 7th, C and G7th. At the core of the passage lie three descents of a whole tone, the melody being shifted down *en bloc.*

I have selected for commentary Rollins's first three choruses as the most representative of his improvising fluency on this occasion.

Chorus I There is no statement here of the original tune of *Three Little Words*. Rollins straightaway invents a brand-new melody, particularly memorable over Bars 1 to 8–a scalar descent with an interesting shuffle of syncopation and stress points. Bars 9 to 16 evidence much of the same satisfying suspension, particularly with the final-beat tie-overs (from Bar 10 into 11, then 14 into 15). These sudden 'blips' in the smooth onward flow are highly rhythmic and totally arresting. The 'middle 8' of the tune (Bars 17 to 24) is treated with a cautious regard for the underlying chords of the original; again, note that 4th-beat suspension between Bars 18 and 19 and the implied 3/4 against 4/4 generated by the reiterated motifs during Bars 20 and 21. And once more Rollins's predilection for cross-bar standstills is evinced between Bars 24 and 25, also 25 and 26.

Chorus II The first 16 bars here (33 to 48) are notable for their fluency and undulating line with some adjustments of the original harmonies (see particularly Bar 45); then, quite out of the blue, over Bars 49 to 51 Rollins substitutes a scalar passage built on the chord of A-flat 7th for the C 7th of the original; a straightforward chromatic descent through bar 52 restores the harmonic *status quo*. Then Bars 57 and 58 contain three chromatically constructed motifs which descend a whole tone at a time to lead into the decoration of the song's own harmony (A-flat 9th) which occupies Bar 60.

Chorus III The first 16 bars (65 to 80) are remarkable for their rhythmic ingenuity and forward-leaning, hustling syncopation–

which, while tending to diffuse the bar lines, in no way diminishes the massive swing of the performance. This constant displacement gives way, at the beginning of the 'middle 8' section (Bars 81 to 84) to a predominantly 'straight' passage of on-the-beat propriety. But the final section parades on Bars 89 to 91 a series of motifs constructed on the whole-tone scale based on C natural, an inspired variation on the song's own C major base at this point.

In sum: which passages most qualify as highspots? The introduction is neat and melodious; after that I would go for the burst of 'new' melody occupying Bars 1 to 16 of Chorus I; the canny tonal shifts of Bars 49 to 58 in Chorus II; and the intriguing fracturing of beat and time during Bars 65-78 in Chorus III–not forgetting that brief excursion into whole-tone rootlessness during Bars 89 to 91!

A performance of sustained, incandescent brilliance: Rollins at his finest.

Ken Rattenbury

It has been noted that some fake scores show differing key structures and we take this opportunity to thank those who took time to draw this to our attention.

St Thomas Pt I

St Thomas Pt 2

St Thomas Pt 3

St Thomas Pt 4

I Know That You Know Pt I

I Know That You Know Pt 2

I Know That You Know Pt 3

Three Little Words Pt I

Three Little Words Pt 2

Three Little Words Pt 3

SONNY ROLLINS: A Skeletal Discography

Sonny Rollins's first recordings took place in 1949; at the time of writing (July 1998) his newest CD – **Global Warming** – has just been released. That adds up to an imposing half-century of recording activity, which means that a full discography of his work would threaten to double the book's length. However, that is not the real reason why I am not offering one.

While it would perhaps be hyperbolic to say that the advent of the CD was the salavation of recorded jazz, there can be no doubt that the effects of that 'revolution' have been enormously beneficial. As detailed in my main text, several major companies have undertaken reissue programmes of comprehensive grandeur and scholarly zeal, and there has been a consonant and equally welcome rise in new recording. One minor consequence of all that has been to put amateur discographers like myself firmly in their place. When I compiled Selective Discographies for my monographs *Oscar Peterson* (1984) and *Stan Getz* (1988) I was not only grateful for Tony Middleton's help: his services were indispensable. But in recent years, discography has become an art apart, one for professionals only: no dilettantés allowed.

Accordingly, those wishing a properly detailed discography are referred to Tom Lord's monumental A - Z work, published by Cadence Jazz Books in Vancouver: the volume which will include Rollins is due for publication in 1998. My 'skeletal discography' here comprises what I hope is a useful chronological listing of album titles. All were made under Rollins's name unless otherwise stated. I have listed labels but not numbers, since these vary according to country and often change anyway. Nearly all records listed are thought to be available in the larger stores and specialist shops. An album that has yet to appear on CD is marked * ; *nas* = not available separately; *oas* = only available separately.

Year	Album	Label
1949	* **Various** - Strictly Bebop	Capitol
	* **Fats Navarro** - Prime Source	Blue Note
	Bud Powell - The Amazing Volume 1	Blue Note
1951-3	Sonny Rollins And The Modern Jazz Quartet.	Prestige
1953	* **Various** - Collector's Item	Esquire
1954	**Miles Davis** - Bags' Groove	Prestige
	Moving Out	Prestige
	Thelonious Monk–Work (aka Thelonious Monk & Sonny Rollins–CD)	Prestige
1955-6	**Clifford Brown** - Complete Emarcy Recordings	Emarcy
1956	Sonny Rollins and Clifford Brown	Prestige
	Sonny Rollins Plus Four	Prestige
	Work Time	Prestige
	Tenor Madness	Prestige
	Saxophone Colossus	Prestige
	Max Roach - Plus Four	Emarcy
	Rollins Plays For Bird	Prestige
	Tour De Force	Prestige
	Sonny Rollins Volume One	Blue Note
	Thelonious Monk - Brilliant Corners	Riverside
1957	Way Out West	Contemporary
	* **Max Roach** - Jazz In 3/4 Time	Emarcy
	Sonny Rollins Volume 2	Blue Note
	The Sound Of Sonny	Riverside
	Newk's Time	Blue Note
	A Night At The Village Vanguard	Blue Note
	Dizzy Gillespie– The Rollins / Stitt Sessions	Verve
1957-8	European Concerts	Bandstand
1957-8	The Complete Sonny Rollins on Blue Note (*nas*) [Collects all five Blue Notes listed above.]	Blue Note
1951-6	The Complete Sonny Rollins on Prestige (7 CDs; *nas*)	Prestige
1958	The Freedom Suite	Riverside

	* Trio / Brass	Verve
	At The Music Inn (with the MJQ)	Atlantic
	Sonny Rollins And the Contemporary Leaders	Contemporary
1959	In Sweden	DIW
1950s	Sonny Rollins And Friends (*pot pourri*)	Verve
1962	The Bridge	RCA
	What's New?	RCA
	Our Man In Jazz	RCA
1963	Three In Jazz	RCA
	Sonny Rollins Meets Coleman Hawkins	RCA
	Rollins Meets Cherry (2 Cds, *oas*)	Moon
1964	Now's The Time	RCA
	The Standard Sonny Rollins	RCA
1962-4	The Alternate Sonny Rollins	RCA
1962-4	The Complete Sonny Rollins on RCA (*nas*) [Collects all eight RCAs listed above.]	RCA
1965	There Will Never Be Another You	Impulse!
	On Impulse!	Impulse!
	Sonny Rollins Trio Live in Europe '65	Magnetic
1966	Alfie	Impulse!
	East Broadway Run Down	Impulse!
1967	In Denmark (2 CDs, *oas*)	Moon
1972	Next Album	Milestone
1973	Horn Culture	Milestone
	Sonny Rollins In Japan	JVC 1974
	The Cutting Edge	Milestone
	First Moves	Jazz Door
1975	Nucleus	Milestone
1976	The Way I Feel	Milestone
1977	Easy Living	Milestone
1978	Don't Stop The Carnival	Milestone
	The Milestone Jazz All Stars In Concert	Milestone
1979	Don't Ask	Milestone
1980	Love At First Sight	Milestone
1981	No Problem	Milestone

1982	Reel Life	Milestone
1984	Sunny Days, Starry Nights	Milestone
1985	The Solo Album	Milestone
1986	G-Man	Milestone
1987	Dancing In The Dark	Milestone
1989	Falling In Love With Jazz	Milestone
1991	Here's To The People	Milestone
1993	Old Flames	Milestone
1995	Sonny Rollins + 3	Milestone
1972-95	Silver City	Milestone
	[2CD *pot pourri* of Rollins's work for Milestone]	
1998	Global Warming	Milestone

Select Bibliography

I have made no attempt to be comprehensive, logging only those books and essays which I consider important and/or have proved valuable during my own research. Anyone wanting a more exhaustive survey is referred to the works listed under Blancq and Kernfield below, which include extensive bibliographies. In addition, with one or two Rollins-related exceptions, I have not included books on other musicians quoted in the main text; the same apples to cited 'non-jazz' works such as Hugh Brogan's *Pelican History of the United States* and James T. Patterson's *Grand Expectations: The United States, 1945-74.*

Bailey, Derek — *Improvisation: Its Nature and Practice in Music (*Ashbourne: Moorland, 1980).

Bailliett, Whitney — *The Sound of Surprise* (Harmondsworth: Penguin, 1963).

Berendt, Joachim — *The Jazz Book* (London: Paladin, 1976).

Blancq, Charles — *Sonny Rollins: the Journey of a Jazzman* (Boston: Twayne, 1983).

Blumenthal, Bob — 'Sonny Rollins', *Down Beat,* xlix / 5 (1982).

Carr, Ian — *Miles Davis* (London: Paladin, 1984).

Carr, Ian; Fairweather, & Priestley, Brian — *Jazz: The Essential Companion* Digby (London: Grafton, 1987).

Chilton, John — The Song of Hawk: The Life and Recordings of Coleman Hawkins (London: Quartet, 1990).

Collier, James Lincoln — *The Making Of Jazz: A Comprehensive History* (London: Macmillan, 1981).

Cook, Richard — 'Sonny Rollins: Return of the Colossus', *Wire,* xviii (1985).

Cook, Richard & Morton, Brian — *The Penguin Guide To Jazz On CD, LP & Cassette* (Harmondsworth: Penguin, 1994).

Cooke, Mervyn — *The Chronicle of Jazz* (London: Thames & Hudson, 1997).

Davis, Francis — *In The Moment: Jazz in the 80s* (New York: Oxford University Press, 1986).

Davis, Miles (with Troupe, Quincy) — *Miles: The Autobiography* (New York: Simon & Schuster, 1989).

Devaux, Scott — The Birth of Bebop (Berkeley: University of California Press, 1997).

Erlywine, Michael (ed) — *All Music Guide To Jazz* (Second Edition; San Francisco: Miller Freeman, 1996).

Feather, Leonard — 'Rollins In 3/4 Time', *Down Beat*, xxiv / 23 (1957).

From Satchmo To Miles (London: Quartet, 1974).

The Jazz Years (London: Quartet, 1986).

The Encyclopedia of Jazz (London: Quartet, 1984).

The Encyclopedia of Jazz in the 60s (London: Quartet, 1976).

The Encyclopedia of Jazz in the 70s (London: Quartet, 1976).

Feather, Leonard & Silvert, Conrad	'Jazz World Remembers Bird', *Down Beat,* xlvii / 8 (1980).
Fordham, John	*Shooting From The Hip* (London: Kyle Cathie, 1996).
	'The Blue Period', *Guardian*, January 23, 1998.
Gauffre, Christian	'What's New, Sonny Rollins?, *Jazzmag,* 414 (1992).
Gayford, Martin	'An Aristocrat of Music and All That Jazz', *Sunday Telegraph*, April 12, 1998.
Giddins, Gary	*Riding On A Blue Note: Jazz & American Pop* (New York: Oxford University Press, 1983).
	Rhythm-a-ning (New York: Oxford University Press, 1986).
Giddins, Gary; Keepnews, Orrin & Stern, Chip	*Silver City*; booklet accompanying Milestone 2-CD 2501-2 (Fantasy Inc, 1996).
Gitler, Ira	'Sonny Rollins: Music Is An Open Sky', *Down Beat*, xxxvi / 11 (1969).
	Swing To Bop (New York: Oxford University Press, 1987).
Goldberg, Joe	*Jazz Masters Of The Fifties* (New York: Macmillan, 1985).
Grime, Kitty	*Jazz At Ronnie Scott's* (London: Hale, 1979).
Harrison, Max; Morgan, Alun; Atkins, Ronald; James, Michael & Cooke, Jack	*Modern Jazz: The Essential Records* (London: Aquarius, 1975).

Hentoff, Nat — 'Sonny Rollins', *Down Beat*, xxiii / 23 (1956).

Jazz Is (New York: Limelight, 1976).

Hentoff Nat & Shapiro, Nat — *Hear Me Talkin To Ya* (London: Penguin, 1962).

Horricks, Raymond (ed) — *These Jazzmen of Our Time* (London: Gollancz, 1960).

Jackson, Michael — *Sonny Rollins: The Search For Self Through Art*. Unpublished dissertation, University of Brighton, 1988.

Jarrett, Michael — 'The Tenor's Vehicle: Reading *Way Out West*'; Krin Gabbard (ed), *Representing Jazz* (Durham: Duke University Press, 1995).

Jeske, Lee — ' Sonny Rollins: The Greatest Jazz Soloist Alive Today', *Jazz Journal International*, xxxii /1 (1979).

Jones, LeRoi — *Blues People* (New York: Morrow, 1968).

Kernfield, Barry (ed) — *The New Grove Dictionary of Jazz* (London: Macmillan, 1988).

Kopulos, Gordon — 'Needed Now: Sonny Rollins', *Down Beat,* xxxviii / 13 (1971).

Larkin, Philip — *All What Jazz* (London: Faber, 1985).

McCarthy, Albert; Morgan, Alun; Oliver, Paul & Harrison, Max — *Jazz On Record: A Critical Guide to the First 50 Years* (London: Hanover, 1968).

McDonough, John — 'On Sonny's Side of the Street', *Down Beat*, lix /12 (1992).

McRae, Barry — *The Jazz Cataclysm* (Letchworth: Aldine, 1967).

The Jazz Handbook (London: Longman, 1987).

'Sonny Rollins', *Jazz Journal*, xviii / 3 (1965).

Meadow, Elliot — 'Rollins Reflects', *Jazz Journal International,* xxxiiii / 6 (1980).

Munton, Alan — 'Misreading Morrison, Mishearing Jazz: A Response to Toni Morrison's Jazz Critics', *Journal of American Studies*, xxxi (1997).

Palmer, Richard — 'Sonny Rollins: Tenor Titan', *Jazz Journal International,* xlv /12 (1992) and xlvi / 2 & 3 (1993).

Porter, Bob — 'This Man Called Sonny Rollins', *Down Beat,* xli / 3 (1974).

Priestley, Brian — 'Max Roach and Sonny at Reading', *Jazz Monthly* xii / 1 (1967).

'Sonny Rollins: Dancing In The Light', *Wire,* lii (1988).

Schoenberg, Loren — *The Complete Sonny Rollins RCA Victor Recordings*; annotation to 6-CD set 09026-68675-2 (New York: BMG, 1997).

Schonfield, Victor — 'Sonny Rollins - Musician' (film review), *Jazz Journal,* xxii / 1 (1969).

Schuller, Gunther — 'Sonny Rollins and the Challenge of Thematic Improvisation', *The Jazz Review*, i/1 (1958).

Shera, Michael — 'Complete RCA Recordings of Sonny Rollins' (record review), *Jazz Journal International*, l /11 (1997).

Sidran, Ben — *Talking Jazz: An Illustrated Oral History* (San Francisco: Pomegranate, 1992).

Taylor, Arthur — *Notes And Tones: Musician-To-Musician Interviews* (London: Quartet, 1983).

Ullman, Michael — *Jazz Lives: Portraits In Words and Pictures* (New York: Perigree, 1980).

Williams, Martin — 'Sonny Rollins', *Jazz Journal,* xix / 7 (1966).

The Jazz Tradition (New York; Oxford University Press, 1983).

Jazz Heritage (New York; Oxford University Press, 1985).

INDEX